Individual
Rights and Civic
Responsibility

THE RIGHTS OF
THE ACCUSED

Fred Ramen

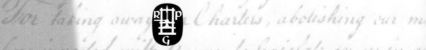

The Rosen Publishing Group, Inc.
New York

Published in 2001 by The Rosen Publishing Group, Inc.
29 East 21st Street, New York, NY 10010

First Edition

Library of Congress Cataloging-in-Publication Data

Ramen, Fred
    Rights of the accused / by Fred Ramen.—1st ed.
        p.   cm. (Individual rights and civic responsibility)
    ISBN 0-8239-3238-9
    1. Criminal procedure—United States—Juvenile literature. 2. Fair trial—United States—Juvenile literature. 3. Due process of law—United States—Juvenile literature. 4. Civil rights—United States—Juvenile literature.[1. United States. Constitution. 1st–10th Amendments. 2. Criminal procedure. 3. Fair trial. 4. Due process of law. 5. Civil rights.] I. Title. II. Series.
    KF9619.6 .R36 2000
    345.73'056—dc21
                                                                00-010646

Manufactured in the United States of America

About the Author

Fred Ramen is a writer and computer programmer who lives in New York City. He is also the author of *Individual Rights and Civic Responsibility: The Right to Freedom from Searches* and two titles—*Influenza* and *Tuberculosis*—in the series Epidemics: Deadly Diseases Throughout History for the Rosen Publishing Group. Fred's interests include the American Civil War, aikido, and the novels of Raymond Chandler. He was a semifinalist in the 1997 *Jeopardy!* Tournament of Champions.

Dedication

For my father, Fred Ramen Jr.

Contents

Introduction

Now over 200 years old, the United States Constitution remains not only the fundamental document of the American experience, but one of the most influential statements on the relationship between a government and the people it governs in human history.

The original text of the Constitution is remarkable in the way it carefully limits the powers of the government, always trying to preserve the greatest amount of liberty possible for the people of the United States. Yet as profound and powerful as the original text is, the first ten amendments to the Constitution—the Bill of Rights—are in many ways even more remarkable.

The authors of the Constitution did not initially believe that a Bill of Rights was necessary or even desirable. They seem to have drafted it in order to fulfill certain promises made to opponents of the original Constitution. Yet their labors produced one of the greatest protectors of human freedom ever created; taken together, the Bill of

Rights has had more influence on the lives of ordinary American citizens than almost any other amendments to the Constitution. Rights guaranteed by it are enjoyed by a citizen every time he or she watches television, goes to church, or attends a school board meeting.

Of particular concern to the authors of the Bill of Rights were the rights of people accused of a crime. The experience of the authors under the British before the Revolutionary War, and their knowledge of the political systems of other countries and from history, had made it clear to them that in order to combat oppression, the criminal justice system must be made as fair and as free from improper government interference as possible. An accused person must be given every possible guarantee of a fair trial; he or she must also be free from the fear of a government prosecuting him or her for political reasons. Also, the government must be restrained as much as possible and prevented from violating the rights of an accused citizen.

So important were these issues to the authors that they wrote several amendments to secure the rights of the accused, namely the Fourth, Fifth, Sixth, and Eighth Amendments. The Fourth Amendment, which covers the kinds of searches and seizures the government is allowed to make, is covered in another book in this series.

The Fifth Amendment covers the guarantee against self-incrimination, the necessity for the government to get an indictment by a grand jury (meaning that a jury of citizens has to decide that enough evidence exists to charge a person with a crime) before trying a person, the right to be tried only once for a crime (the double jeopardy clause), and the guarantee that the government will give an accused

(Copy of the first Draught by G. M.)

A Declaration of Rights made by the Representatives of the good People of Virginia, assembled in full and free Convention; which Rights do pertain to them and their Posterity, as the Basis and Foundation of Government.

1. That all men are created equally free & independent, & have certain inherent natural Rights, of which they can not, by any Compact, deprive or divest their Posterity; among which are the Enjoyment of Life & Liberty, with the Means of acquiring & possessing Property, & pursuing & obtaining Happiness & Safety.

2. That all Power is by God & Nature vested in, & consequently derived from the People; that Magistrates are their Trustees & Servants, and at all Times amenable to them.

3. That Government is or ought to be instituted for the common Benefit, Protection & Security of the People, Nation or Community. Of all the various Modes & Forms of Government that is best, which is capable of producing the greatest Degree of Happiness & Safety, & is most effectually secured against the Danger of mal Administration; and that whenever any Government shall be found inadequate or contrary to these purposes, a majority of the Community hath an indubitable, unalienable & indefeasible Right, to reform, alter, or abolish it, in such

---

Several of the constitutional amendments that make up the Bill of Rights are concerned with the rights of the accused.

person a full and fair trial (the due process clause). The Fifth Amendment also guarantees the government will not take land or property from a person without compensating the person for it. This is not a right of the accused and so is not addressed in this book.

The Sixth Amendment guarantees a speedy trial with an impartial jury composed of people from the region the crime was committed in, guarantees the accused person the right to confront the people accusing him or her and the witnesses to the crime, guarantees that the accused will have the ability to bring witnesses for his or her defense, and guarantees the right of that person to have a lawyer (counsel) to assist in his or her defense. These are some of the most important rights an accused person has, and they have been the source of several important and controversial Supreme Court decisions over the last seventy years.

The Eighth Amendment guarantees that bail (an amount of money put up by an accused person to gain release from jail and forfeited if he or she does not show up for trial) will not be excessive, that any fines imposed by the court will not be excessive, and that no cruel or unusual punishments will be inflicted. With the exception of the last, which was used for a time to prevent the execution of convicted criminals throughout the United States, these rights have not been the source of many important Supreme Court decisions.

This remarkable series of rights has become the foundation of the modern trial system. From the simple text of the Bill of Rights, the Supreme Court has created an intricate, tightly controlled system dedicated to the principle that a person must not only be given every opportunity to prove his or her innocence, but that in order to hand down a punishment, the government must disprove that innocence beyond any reasonable doubt. This delicate balance between accused and accuser, citizen and government, has frequently become the source of controversy, and it has always been difficult to determine exactly how the balance should be maintained. But for 200 years, the Bill of Rights, and behind it the U.S. Constitution, has served as a guiding principle for those charged with the enormous duty of protecting the rights of American citizens.

But why do we have a Constitution, or a Bill of Rights? Why did the remarkable people behind the American Revolution feel the need to create a document that precisely laid out the functions of the national government? Why did they choose the form that the Constitution eventually took? How has our interpretation of their vision changed over the two centuries since the Constitution was ratified? What do the Constitution and the Bill of Rights really mean?

The answers to the first three questions can be found in the next few chapters. The rest of this book deals with the answers—if they exist—to the last two questions. But in a larger sense, there is no one way to say what the Constitution means. Its meaning is changing every day, as Americans continue to redefine exactly what its most important idea—liberty for all people—means to them today.

1 Origins of the United States Constitution

The Constitution, in many ways, is a radical document. In simple, everyday speech, it sets forth not only the structure of the United States government but what the powers of that government are—mostly by describing what the government is forbidden to do. Its simplicity and concern with the preservation of the liberty of the citizens of the United States make it a unique document today; and when it was first written, in 1787, it was truly astonishing. Yet the Constitution has important predecessors, some thousands of years old, that influenced the thinking of the men who sat down to consider how they would design their "more perfect union."

Both the ancient Greeks and Romans had long traditions of government that included at least some representation by the people being governed. Ancient Athens, for example, was governed directly by an assembly composed of all the citizens of the city. Codes of law and basic constitutions were drafted by Athens and several other Greek

11

The Romans developed the idea of making written law accessible to all citizens. The emperor Justinian collected Roman law into the famous and influential Code of Justinian.

cities; the Greek philosopher Aristotle collected many of them for a study of government. Ancient Rome, during the Republic period, had many elected assemblies and officials. The Romans also evolved the concept of making the written law of Rome accessible to all citizens; special wooden tablets with the laws engraved on them were on public display at the center of the city. Even during the Roman Empire, written law codes remained important; the emperor of the Eastern Roman Empire, Justinian, collected and revised Roman law into the famous Code of Justinian, the influence of which can still be seen in the laws of many European nations today.

During the Middle Ages, however, ordinary people lost much of their voice in government. Kings and other nobles governed directly, if not absolutely. But as cities became more important during the Middle Ages, documents called charters began to change the relationships between the nobles and the people they governed. Basically, a charter relieved people in a certain region, such as a city, from obligations they owed to a noble in return for other considerations. For example, it was common to have to serve in a local noble's military forces for a period of time each year, which was inconvenient for merchants and shop owners. A charter might be granted by the noble exempting people from this service in return for money or manufactured goods. From these simple origins, charters grew into very complex statements on what the exact obligations each side owed the other.

The most important charter in English history was the Magna Carta (Latin for "great charter") issued by King John to his barons in 1215. This charter was important for several reasons. First, it was not simply granted by the king but

13

was demanded by his subjects. Second, it made many reforms to the justice system to protect the rights of the English and to make the system more fair. Perhaps most important, it set out definite limits to the king's power, and warned him that if he violated the charter, the barons had the right to rebel and try to remove him. Although the Magna Carta actually did little to help the common people of England (it was, after all, written by the nobility to protect themselves from the king), its principle—to limit the power of government and to guarantee certain rights— became the central idea of English law.

This kind of tradition can be seen in the other great statement of British law, the 1689 English Bill of Rights. This law completely changed the balance of power in English government, for in order for a king or queen to lawfully come to power, he or she had to accept all of its conditions. It essentially prevented a British monarch from acting without the consent of Parliament, the British legislature; it also provided for free elections and freedom of speech for members of Parliament and prevented the king or queen from changing or disallowing laws Parliament had created. Even more important, however, was the idea behind the English Bill of Rights, for it meant that English people were not the subjects of a king or queen who could rule absolutely but people who had a voice in their own government and would not consent to live under a tyrant. It was precisely this pride in the idea of the "rights of an Englishman" that caused the great conflict between the American colonists and the British government.

The American colonies also had charters. In many places, these charters gave them even greater freedom than

England's Magna Carta was issued in 1215. It limited the power of the monarchy and made the justice system fairer.

what the English people enjoyed. Almost all the colonies had legislatures that were free to enact laws for the colonists; many colonies also specifically granted freedom of worship, making these colonies attractive to religious minorities in England who were oppressed by the government. Thus, when the British government began to insist that it had supreme power over the colonists, and even began to revoke the charters of some of the colonies, it seemed only natural for the colonists to demand their rights as British subjects and, eventually, to invoke the right to rebel that the Magna Carta had outlined.

In United States history, the Declaration of Independence has a role similar to the Magna Carta. Not a legally binding document, it nevertheless sets forth the basic principles of American liberty in clear, precise terms, and it has served as the guiding light for American government ever since.

Similarly, the Virginia Bill of Rights, issued in 1776, served as a model for the United States Bill of Rights, calling for the right to trial by jury, the requirement of search warrants, and freedom of the press, among other rights.

Even during the Revolution, the colonies—now states—began to draft constitutions to guarantee the rights for which they were fighting. All of them called for government by elected legislatures, and many had broad guarantees of rights similar to those granted by Virginia. Some of these would become models for the U.S. Constitution. What is most striking, however, is the need the colonists felt to create documents that would set forth precisely the powers (and limits on that power) of government, providing a solid basis for deciding on the legality of any law or act of government.

The Articles of Confederation

Yet strangely enough, when the Revolution was won and the colonists had gained their independence, they did not create a national government along the lines of the various state constitutions. Instead, in the Articles of Confederation, they created a national government with almost no power. The Articles instead provided for a loose organization of the states, providing a way for them to deal with questions of national importance, such as war, and generally leaving all other questions, including the idea of fundamental rights, up to the individual states. There were several weaknesses with the arrangement. The national government had no power to tax the country in order to support itself, but instead had to ask each state to contribute the necessary money; however, it lacked the power to enforce even these

What Is Federalism?

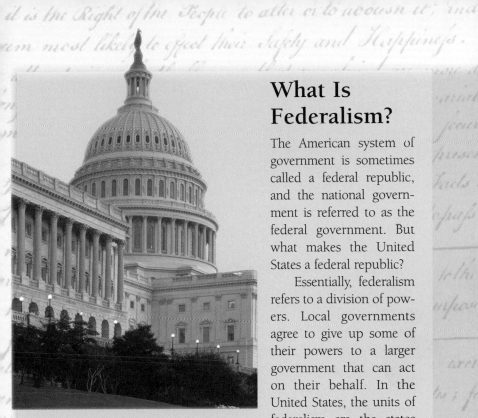

The American system of government is sometimes called a federal republic, and the national government is referred to as the federal government. But what makes the United States a federal republic?

Essentially, federalism refers to a division of powers. Local governments agree to give up some of their powers to a larger government that can act on their behalf. In the United States, the units of federalism are the states and the national, or federal, government.

The Constitution makes clear this basic division. The federal government is given certain powers—the right to coin money, to declare war, to regulate commerce between the states—that each state is forbidden to do. But the Constitution gave only very specific powers to the federal government. All other matters were to be left to the states.

Tension between the states and the federal government has been a constant issue before the Supreme Court. To this day, the theory known as states' rights holds that the federal government should interfere as little as possible with the states. On the other hand, many of the reforms sought by the civil rights movement of the 1960s were possible only when the federal government prevented the states from discriminating against their own citizens.

One of this book's major themes is the story of how federal power gradually extended the protections of the Bill of Rights to all citizens of the United States.

17

requests. Each state could coin its own money; also, each state could put taxes, called duties and tariffs, on products imported into them from other states. There was no executive branch charged with enforcing the laws, making it difficult to ensure that even the limited powers of Congress would be respected. Any changes to the Articles required the consent of all the states, making it easy for one state to block necessary changes.

These defects endangered the very existence of the United States in the first few years after the Revolution. There was a very real danger that the government might collapse, leaving a loose collection of weak republics along the eastern coast of North America. Because of this danger, a movement arose calling for a stronger and more stable national government that would address the faults of the Articles of Confederation. The stage was set for the Constitutional Convention of 1787.

2 The Constitutional Convention

In 1787, after a strongly worded report, supposedly written by New York's Alexander Hamilton, who was a leading critic of the Articles of Confederation, Congress issued a call for a convention that would meet to revise the Articles. The convention would quickly move past its limited goal of revising and write a document that not only would replace the existing Articles but change the entire theory of the government of the United States.

Each state except for Rhode Island sent a delegation to the convention. Many of the members were some of the ablest men of their generation. Thirty-nine of the fifty-five delegates had served in Congress; there were eight signers of the Declaration of Independence, more than thirty veterans of the Revolutionary War, and all were experienced in the government of their home states. The major participants, however, were New York's Alexander Hamilton; Pennsylvania's James Wilson and Gouveneur Morris, who was eventually responsible for the Constitution's opening

19

The Constitutional Convention met in 1787 to revise the Articles of Confederation. George Washington (far right) came out of retirement to preside over the convention.

phrase, "We the People"; and Virginia's James Madison, the principal architect of the Constitution and, eventually, the Bill of Rights. George Washington came out of retirement to serve as the convention's president.

Three major problems confronted the conventioneers. First was the question of representation in the national government, of finding a way to protect the small states and yet give the big states an appropriate voice. Second was creating an executive branch that would be able to adequately enforce national law. Finally, they needed to find a way to resolve the many economic problems resulting from the original Articles of Confederation. Each problem caused a lengthy debate before a compromise suitable to all could be reached.

The first problem was solved by the decision to have two separate houses of Congress: the House of Representatives, where representation would be based on the population of each state, and the Senate, where each state would have two representatives. Each house was given different powers to help balance each other: the Senate, among other things, confirms Supreme Court justices, confirms cabinet members, and ratifies treaties; the House, on the other hand, controls tax laws and breaks ties in presidential elections. This kind of careful balancing is typical of the principle of checks and balances, where each power given to a branch of government is balanced by the ability of another branch of government to stop that power.

Some of the best examples of these checks and balances can be seen in how the convention solved the second of their major problems, the creation of an executive branch. They needed to give the president enough power that he could enforce the nation's laws, but not so much that he could become a tyrant. The answer was to split powers between him and Congress. The president is the commander-in-chief of all U.S. armed forces, but only Congress can start a war or provide funds for the military; the president can veto a law Congress passes, but Congress can override his veto with enough votes. In this way, the delegates were satisfied that they had created an executive branch that would not be permitted to become tyrannical, although, as we shall see, many people continued to feel that the president was too strong.

The last of the three problems was perhaps the easiest to resolve. Congress was given the ability to tax the entire nation. States were forbidden to coin their own money, and Congress was given the power to regulate commerce between them. In this way, they prevented the trade wars that had developed between several of the states during the Confederate period.

In addition to the legislative (Congress) and executive (the president) branches of government, the Constitution provided for the powers of a judicial branch—the Supreme Court. The powers initially given to the Supreme Court were somewhat limited. It decided cases between different states, or between the United States government and the governments of the states or foreign nations; but soon after the ratification of the Constitution, the Supreme Court would come into its own by asserting perhaps its most important power: deciding whether or not a law was constitutional.

The Constitution in its original form has remarkably little to say about the rights of citizens of the United States. It does forbid the granting of noble titles and the passage of laws that make something a crime after the act has been

The Amendment Process

Article V of the U.S. Constitution lays out the procedures for amending, or changing, the Constitution. There are two ways that this can be accomplished. The first way is for two thirds of each house of Congress (pictured at left) to approve an amendment and send it to the state legislatures to be ratified. The second way, which has never actually happened, is for two-thirds of the state legislatures to call for a convention to write new amendments; this would be almost the same as calling a new constitutional convention.

In either case, the new amendment must be approved by three-fourths of the state legislatures. Once that has happened, the amendment is a part of the Constitution, and only another amendment may change it.

The original Constitution prior to 1808 forbade any amendments that threatened slavery. Only one amendment has specifically repealed another amendment (the Twenty-first Amendment it repealed the Eighteenth Amendment, which had made alcoholic beverages illegal in the United States), although many amendments have had effects on other amendments. The most important example in this book is the effect of the Fourteenth Amendment on the original ten amendments, the Bill of Rights.

committed (*ex post facto* laws) or laws that pass judgment on a person without a trial (bills of attainder). Also, the right to trial by jury was guaranteed. Although some of the delegates argued for including a statement on the basic rights of citizens, the majority felt that the rights of the people were protected merely by forbidding the government to do so many things.

While the Constitution was in many ways superior to the Articles of Confederation, it still provoked a firestorm of criticism during the debate on its ratification. Some charged that the convention had acted illegally in deciding to radically change the structure of government, rather than just modifying the existing Articles. Many felt that the states lost too much power under the Constitution. Still others feared that the new government, and especially the president, would be too powerful and oppress the people. It had, after all, been only eleven years since the start of the Revolution, and many people were suspicious of any central authority.

The two sides gradually became known as the Federalists, who were in favor of the Constitution and a strong central government, and the Antifederalists, who opposed the Constitution and disliked a strong central government. Alexander Hamilton, James Madison, and John Jay were leaders of the Federalist cause; their essays, collected as the Federalist Papers, are brilliant arguments in favor of the Constitution and did much to swing public opinion to the side of the Federalists.

The debate over ratification was most intense in the big states of Virginia, Massachusetts, and New York. Massachusetts narrowly ratified the Constitution only after it was decided to recommend a number of Antifederalist amendments to it; in Virginia, James Madison led the Federalist cause to a narrow victory by promising to consider a bill of rights that would be added to the Constitution. With Virginia and Massachusetts in line, New York soon followed. Although it would take more than two years for the last two states—North Carolina and Rhode Island—to ratify the Constitution, the decision of the three largest and most important states to support the Constitution made its eventual ratification inevitable. The Constitution was now the law of the land.

James Madison, despite sometimes intense opposition in Virginia, managed to be elected to the House of Representatives. Once there, he began work on a series of amendments to the Constitution that would become the Bill of Rights, even though at the Constitutional Convention he had argued that such a bill was unnecessary. Yet despite his earlier opposition, he turned to the task with great skill and efficiency, creating a legacy of liberty still enjoyed by U.S. citizens today.

3 The Birth of the Bill of Rights

James Madison originally proposed, and got the House of Representatives to approve, seventeen amendments to the Constitution. The Senate failed to approve the last five; of the twelve that were sent to the states, only ten achieved ratification right away. Originally, Madison wanted the amendments to be inserted directly into the Constitution, but it was decided instead to place them at the end of the document and call them the Bill of Rights.

The Bill of Rights is unusual in that most of the amendments do not either strike down an existing power of the government or grant it new powers. Rather, they speak specifically to what the government cannot do. They are thus in keeping with the way Madison wrote the original Constitution.

While it may seem completely sensible to us today that the Constitution should make a basic statement on the rights of U.S citizens, the Federalists had several arguments as to why they had not done so in the original document.

One reason was that they felt that it was the states, not the federal government, that would be the principal guardians of the rights of the people. This was an especially useful argument to make against those who felt that the states were losing too much power to the central government.

Others feared that if specific rights were mentioned in the Constitution, the government might take away those not mentioned in it. These fears led to the inclusion of the Ninth and Tenth Amendments to the Constitution.

However, by 1789, Madison was convinced that the Constitution required amendments protecting certain civil rights that were necessary in order to have a working democracy. The Bill of Rights, of which he was the chief architect, reflects this belief in fundamental civil rights.

The First Amendment, for example, guarantees the right to freedom of speech, assembly, and religion—all the vital needs of a varied and democratic population, especially the rights of free speech and assembly.

The Second and Third Amendments recall the colonists' struggle against the British, preserving the right to bear arms and guaranteeing freedom from the housing of troops among civilians in peacetime. Violations of these principles had been among some of the most detested acts of the British during the period before the Revolution.

The Fourth through Sixth Amendments, which were discussed in the introduction, deal with the rights of the accused in a criminal trial (except the "takings" clause of the Fifth Amendment, which prevents the government from taking a person's property without appropriate payment).

The Seventh Amendment guarantees the right to a trial by jury in civil cases where the amount sought is greater than $20. The Eighth Amendment, also detailed in the introduction, prohibits cruel and unusual punishment.

The Ninth and Tenth Amendments note that just because the Bill of Rights listed certain rights, these should not be understood to be the only rights of citizens of the United States, and that any powers not specifically given to the federal government (or denied to the states) by the Constitution are retained by the states or the people of the United States. Neither of these amendments has been the source of many court cases, although as guiding principles they remain important in our interpretation of the Constitution and the Bill of Rights.

It should be noted here that the intent of the Bill of Rights was primarily to protect the majority from the minority. In other words, the Bill of Rights protects the rights of the people from encroachment by the government. The fear of the generation that fought the Revolution and wrote the Constitution was not so much that an individual or small minority might be deprived of their individual rights, but that a tyrannical central government would rob the people as a whole of their rights. This had been the perception by the colonists of the actions of the British government before the Revolution. The Antifederalists' demands for a bill of rights had been founded in this fear of a tyrannical government, and the wording of the Bill of Rights seeks to calm their fears. The language of the Bill of Rights, with its heavy use of negatives, is much more concerned with prohibiting the government from interfering with the rights of the people than in asserting what those rights are. To many political thinkers of the day, the "rights of the people" were a natural part of being alive; thus Thomas Jefferson had said

James Madison

James Madison (1751–1836) was one of the most important figures in early U.S. history. In addition to being one of the principal authors of the Constitution and the Bill of Rights, he was at various times a congressman, secretary of state, and president of the United States. He was a member of Congress under the original Articles of Confederation; his firsthand observation of the weakness of the national government led him to push for the Constitutional Convention.

Madison was the chief architect of the large-state Virginia plan, but he compromised his ideas to produce the original Constitution. His efforts helped gain the crucial ratification of the Constitution by Virginia. During the debate, he promised to introduce a bill of rights to the Constitution, which he did as a member of the first Congress. He later served as Thomas Jefferson's secretary of state, where he became indirectly involved in the famous *Marbury v. Madison* case.

Madison was elected president in 1808 and 1812. During his second term, the United States fought and won the War of 1812. After his tenure as president, he retired to Virginia, where he worked to end slavery and helped run the University of Virginia.

Madison's notes on the Constitutional Convention are our best source of information on the writing of the Constitution to this day. The great Kentucky senator Henry Clay called him, after George Washington, "our greatest statesman."

that people were possessed of "inalienable" rights (such as life, liberty, and the pursuit of happiness) that no government could deny existed.

But while the overall construction of the Bill of Rights was designed to shield the people from the government, in the area of the rights of the accused, where one person has the entire government pitted against him or her, the Bill of Rights speaks to the rights of the individual. Yet even here we find that the Bill of Rights was designed more to prevent the government from constructing an engine of tyranny than to guarantee rights to individuals. Even the Fifth Amendment's guarantee against self-incrimination has less to do with an individual's right not to speak than with the government's ability to compel a person to provide evidence against himself or herself.

Yet in the over 200 years since the adoption of the Bill of Rights, there has been a shift in how it has been interpreted. No longer is the Bill of Rights primarily a protection for the people against the government; now it frequently functions as a shield for the rights of individuals. Instead of merely preventing the government from taking a course of action, the Bill of Rights can now make it take a course of action. To understand how this revolution came about—easily one of the most far-reaching changes in American political life—we will first examine how the Bill of Rights was initially understood and how the events of the Civil War forever changed notions of freedom in the United States.

The Lost Amendment

"No law, varying the compensation for the services of the Senators and Representatives, shall take effect, until an election of Representatives shall have intervened."

Thus reads the most recent amendment to the U.S. Constitution, the Twenty-seventh Amendment (ratified May 7, 1992). Yet this amendment is actually older than the Bill of Rights, having been proposed one day before the First Amendment.

The Twenty-seventh Amendment was part of Madison's original Bill of Rights. However, it was not originally approved by enough states and so did not receive ratification at that time.

This amendment prevents Congress from giving itself a pay raise before the next election. That is, if Congress votes a pay increase, it cannot take effect before an election—and if the voters think the increase is excessive, they can vote the members of Congress out of office!

In the 1980s, a young Texan discovered the lost amendment and began a campaign for its ratification. In 1992, it was announced that forty states had ratified it, making it a part of the Constitution.

This sparked controversy, since several of the states that ratified it did so in the 1790s. However, the Supreme Court has ruled that a state cannot withdraw its ratification if there is nothing in the text of the amendment that gives a definite period in which its ratification has to take place. Thus, the long-lost amendment was finally allowed to become part of the supreme law of the land.

4 The Supreme Court and the Bill of Rights Before the Civil War

The United States Supreme Court is the judicial branch of the federal government. It alone has the authority to deal with disputes between two states, or a state and the federal government. It is also the court of final appeal for the lower federal courts. Yet it is not this rather limited power that makes the Supreme Court so important. Rather, it is the power of judicial review, the ability to decide that a law does not comply with the Constitution and must therefore be stricken down, that has become the power most often associated with the Supreme Court.

Judicial review is not a power assigned to the Supreme Court by the Constitution. Its existence owes much to one extremely powerful and influential chief justice, John Marshall.

Marshall was the fourth chief justice of the Supreme Court and served longer in that position than anyone else. During his time as chief justice, he issued rulings in three cases that had profound effects on how the courts interpreted the U.S. Constitution.

The first of these was the case that established the principle of judicial review, *Marbury v. Madison* (1803). William Marbury had been appointed as justice of the peace for the District of Columbia by President John Adams shortly before he was replaced in office by Thomas Jefferson. When the new secretary of state, James Madison—the same Madison who wrote the Bill of Rights—failed to give Marbury the job, Marbury went directly to the Supreme Court, asking it to compel Madison into giving him the job, as the Judiciary Act of 1789 allowed.

Marshall—ironically enough, the former secretary of state under Adams who had for unknown reasons failed to complete Marbury's appointment in the first place—ruled that the Constitution did not allow him to order Madison to give Marbury the job, despite what the Judiciary Act said. Then, in a bold move, Marshall declared that that part of the act was unconstitutional and must be stricken. Furthermore, only the judicial branch had the authority to decide whether a law was constitutional.

Marshall's basis for this decision was the supremacy clause of the Constitution (Article VI), which makes the Constitution the supreme law of the land, and valid even though a state or federal law could contradict it. Prior to Marshall's decision, the exact mechanism of enforcing the supremacy clause had not been settled upon. Thomas Jefferson and others who wanted the states to have little interference from the federal government held that the individual states should nullify (strike down) unconstitutional laws. Others felt that juries would be the main way to prevent unconstitutional laws, by refusing to convict people accused of breaking a law they felt was unconstitutional.

33

Marshall, however, was a staunch Federalist who believed in a strong central government. His doctrine of judicial review brilliantly kept the power to review a law within the federal government, while making sure that its power rested with the impartial judicial branch.

The force of Marshall's personality and his long service as chief justice helped to reinforce his ideas and make them the official policies of the federal government. Two other cases decided by Marshall also had enormous influence, one until the present day, and one until the Civil War. The first of these, *Martin v. Hunter's Lessee* (1816), was another victory for defenders of a strong central government. The main matter in the case concerned whether or not state judges in Virginia could decide if a law violated the U.S. Constitution. Marshall ruled that they could not. This was crucial because it kept the Constitution from being interpreted in different ways in different states—as would have been the case had the Virginia judges had their way.

The second case, *Barron v. Baltimore 1833*, explains why there are so few cases concerning the Bill of Rights decided by the Supreme Court before the Civil War. John Barron had owned a wharf that the city of Baltimore had taken from him in a public-works project. Barron then applied to the Supreme Court for compensation under the "takings" clause of the Fifth Amendment, arguing that as a U.S. citizen he was entitled to its protection.

The court ruled against him. Marshall held that the Bill of Rights did not apply to action taken by the states, just the federal government. His reasoning was that the Bill of Rights limited only powers granted to the federal government, which clearly did not include the city of Baltimore.

Structure of the Supreme Court and the Judiciary Act of 1789

The Constitution does not say how many justices should sit on the Supreme Court; however, it gives Congress the power to decide the issue. In the Judiciary Act of 1789, Congress decided there should be six people on the Supreme Court: a chief justice and five associate justices. Each of them must be approved by the Senate before he or she can become a Supreme Court justice. Once approved, though, this person serves for life or until he or she wishes to retire—or is impeached and convicted. If an associate justice is nominated to become chief justice, he or she must again be approved by the Senate. This happened most recently in 1986, when associate justice William H. Rehnquist became chief justice.

The number of justices Congress established in 1789 did not stay the same. While there has always been only one chief justice, Congress kept increasing the number of associate justices: to six in 1807, eight in 1837, and nine in 1864—making a total of ten justices on the Supreme Court bench, the most of any period. In 1866, this number was reduced to nine following a vacancy on the Court, where it has stayed ever since.

The first black man to sit on the Supreme Court was Thurgood Marshall, who served from 1967 to 1991. The first woman to sit on the bench was Sandra Day O'Connor (pictured above), who was confirmed in 1981.

Furthermore, he argued—probably correctly—that the Bill of Rights was created to protect the public from oppression by the federal government, not the states.

Marshall's decision effectively closed off any appeals under the Bill of Rights for actions that took place because of state or city acts. While the federal government could not violate any of the provisions of the Bill of Rights, the states clearly could. This was not really a major concern because many states had their own bills of rights, which in some cases granted even greater rights than the federal Bill of Rights. Yet the potential existed for great injustices to be committed, and many were, at both the state and federal level. Racial, ethnic, and religious prejudice existed in many places, supported by local laws.

Marshall's interpretation of the Bill of Rights was impeccable and totally in keeping with the Constitution as written. Yet while it was legal, it did little to help the victims of local laws who were powerless to gain the protections that the Bill of Rights seemed to promise. Meanwhile, too, the young republic was being torn apart over the issue of slavery—its economics, morality, extension, and very existence. The result of those tensions was the Civil War, and it was to have a profound influence on the nature of the U.S. Constitution and on the Bill of Rights.

5

The Fourteenth Amendment and the Bill of Rights

The Civil War (1861–1865) was a devastating conflict. Over 600,000 soldiers died during the war, along with thousands of civilians. Millions of dollars of property damage was inflicted on the South, which was so economically devastated that it took decades to recover.

The Civil War also changed the way that a person related to the federal government. Before the war, about the only times a person would have dealings with the central government was when voting or mailing a letter. But the war, with its massive requirements for soldiers, ammunition, food, and transport, changed all that. Millions of young men were directly employed by the government as soldiers. Others went to work as contractors for the government, supplying it with war materials. In some areas, martial law was declared, meaning that the people there were directly governed by the federal government (through the army).

The central issues of the Civil War were in many ways constitutional and similar to the ones that had divided the

37

Following the Civil War, the Thirteenth, Fourteenth, and Fifteenth Amendments outlawed slavery and protected the rights of former slaves. This cartoon depicts a freed slave being intimidated while trying to vote.

Constitutional Convention. The Southern states, with their smaller populations and dependence on a farming economy, pushed for a weak central government that did not interfere with the states. They repeatedly blocked attempts by Northern interests to increase federal involvement with state projects, as well as tariff laws that would have helped to protect the growing industry of the Northern states.

The Civil War, however, forever changed that balance. Many of the Southern states were placed under direct federal control, including occupation by the army, after the war. The cause of the war, the issue of secession—the ability of a state to leave the Union—was decided against the states. But it was the heart of the difference between the North and South—slavery—that would prompt Congress to forever change the way the Constitution and the Bill of Rights operated.

President Abraham Lincoln's Emancipation Proclamation (1863) had freed all slaves in the portion of the Confederacy that was not occupied by Union troops at that time. This did not, however, include slaves in areas occupied by the Union or slaves in states that remained in the Union, such as Maryland. Even before the war ended, however, Congress was working on a series of amendments—the Reconstruction amendments—that would not only outlaw slavery but attempt to bring justice to all citizens of the United States.

The first of these amendments, the Thirteenth Amendment, outlawed slavery throughout the United States. The last, the Fifteenth Amendment, made all persons born within the United States able to vote, regardless of race or color. However, the most far-reaching of the

Reconstruction amendments was the Fourteenth Amendment, the "due process" amendment.

With the passage of the Thirteenth Amendment, millions of slaves became free citizens overnight. However, there remained the problem of how to integrate them into society. The former slaves were likely to be the targets of extreme prejudice wherever they went. Furthermore, the states that had held them in slavery could hardly be considered likely to try and defend their rights. However, the federal government could do little to protect them: As the Supreme Court had ruled in *Barron v. Baltimore* (see chapter 4), even the Bill of Rights did not apply to actions taken by a state against its citizens.

The solution was the Fourteenth Amendment. The amendment consists of five sections. The second through fourth sections deal with the situation after the Civil War. Respectively, they change the method of counting people in a state (for purposes of representation in the House of Representatives) from counting slaves as three-fifths of a person to counting each free person as a whole person; make it illegal for former Confederates to hold federal office; and refuse to honor the debts of the Confederacy. The last section gives Congress the power to write laws to enforce the provisions of the amendment. But it is the first section of the amendment that is the most important.

Section one contains three very important changes to the Constitution. First, all persons born or naturalized in the United States are citizens of the United States. Second, a state is forbidden to restrict the rights and privileges of U.S. citizens. Third, each state must guarantee "due process" before depriving a person of his or her life, liberty,

Appeals and the Supreme Court

The Supreme Court primarily resolves issues between states, or between the United States and foreign powers. What makes the Court so powerful in interpreting the nation's laws, however, is its power to review appeals.

In order to hear an appeal, a federal court must decide that there is a "federal question" involved in the case. A federal question is one that relates to an act of Congress, a treaty, or a constitutional question. Since the adoption of the Fourteenth Amendment, many cases have been heard under the federal question, to what degree does a right contained in the Bill of Rights also apply to the states?

Since 1925, most cases come to the Supreme Court by means of a writ of certiorari, which is a petition that the losing side can file with the Court asking it to review a lower court's decision. If four justices vote to hear the case, the Court will decide the matter.

Each side will then prepare papers, or briefs, that detail the reasons why the original decision should be overturned or stay the same, and list cases that provide precedents for that decision. Each side also gets the chance to speak before the Court. At the end of the process, the justices consider the arguments and then take a vote. The decision of the majority becomes the final decision. The majority must, and the minority may, then prepare a statement, called an opinion, explaining the reasons they voted the way they did.

or property. Furthermore, each state must provide "equal protection" under its laws for any citizen.

The purpose of these radical changes was to protect the former slaves. First, it clearly made them U.S. citizens, despite having formerly been slaves. Second, and perhaps most important, it guaranteed every citizen of any state the rights belonging to a U.S. citizen. In time, this would be understood to include the Bill of Rights, although it would take almost a century for this change to occur. The final two changes were to protect the former slaves from being treated unfairly by the state governments (due process) and to prevent laws discriminating against them (equal protection).

But more than serving to protect the former slaves, the Fourteenth Amendment was the start of a process of radically changing the federal government's relationship with its citizens. No longer would a citizen be able to spend most of his or her time not interacting with the federal government; many temporary measures taken by the government during the war (such as income tax) would eventually become a permanent part of the government's structure. Some of this had to do with the ultimate failure of the extreme states' rights position that had led to the threat of secession and the Civil War, but there was also a rising feeling of nationalism in the United States that changed how people saw their country. Prior to the war, a person was likely to consider his or her home state his or her "country." In fact, up until the war, the United States was considered to be a plural noun: "the United States are." After the war, when millions of people had moved all over the country, reaching places they had never dreamed of seeing, that changed. The United States became singular, a single nation: "the United States is."

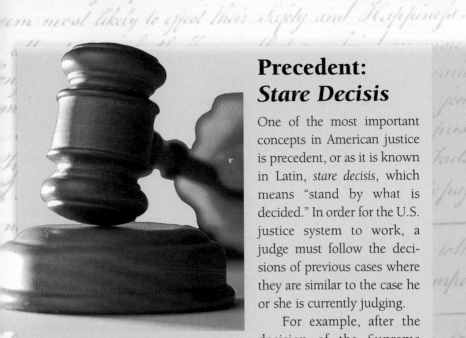

Precedent: *Stare Decisis*

One of the most important concepts in American justice is precedent, or as it is known in Latin, *stare decisis*, which means "stand by what is decided." In order for the U.S. justice system to work, a judge must follow the decisions of previous cases where they are similar to the case he or she is currently judging.

For example, after the decision of the Supreme Court in *Miranda v. Arizona* (see chapter 6), which requires that the police clearly inform a suspect of his or her constitutional rights when that person is arrested, a judge in any case where a suspect was not read his or her rights would have to throw out any evidence that resulted from the arrest, and possibly the judge might have to throw out the entire case.

The Supreme Court, however, is not bound by its own precedents. It may decide to ignore precedent and decide similar cases differently. This new decision then becomes precedent for the lower courts. The Supreme Court does not reverse itself often or without much consideration. When it does, it usually justifies doing so for a number of reasons. It may decide that the current case is significantly different from the earlier case; in such cases, the precedent may not change, as the ruling was strictly concerned with the current case. On the other hand, the Court may decide that the original ruling was a mistake and that the current ruling is correct; this may be because of changes to the nation since the original decision or faulty reasoning by the original Court.

43

The eradication of slavery and the extension of the rights of all U.S. citizens also signaled the start of a movement to bring greater freedom to all people throughout the nation. The country was to become more democratic, continuing to expand the right to vote and pushing for reforms that strengthened the rights of the individual. Unfortunately, many had to wait decades before the real power of the Fourteenth Amendment would finally be used to protect their rights.

The Rights of the Accused Since the Civil War

Although the Fourteenth Amendment paved the way for the extension of the Bill of Rights to the states, the actual process of doing so took many years. This is primarily because of the conservative nature of the court during the later part of the nineteenth century. During this time, the Fourteenth Amendment was used primarily by businesses seeking the same protections from states as individuals received.

It was not until the twentieth century that many of the rights guaranteed in the Bill of Rights were held to apply to the states as well. This process, called incorporation, was a slow one, frequently requiring the reversal of previous Supreme Court rulings. Some rights have never been incorporated against the states. The Second Amendment right to bear arms is one example; the Third Amendment freedom from the quartering of troops with civilians in peacetime has never been the basis of any Supreme Court decision.

The following chapters examine the rights a person accused of a crime has under the Bill of Rights. (The Fifth and Sixth Amendments are closely linked, so the first of the Sixth Amendment chapters also discusses the Fifth Amendment requirement that an indictment be presented.)

As the federal government expanded its power and influence, the Court likewise expanded its interpretation of the Bill of Rights. During the intense debates over civil rights in the 1950s and 60s, the Court used the Fourteenth Amendment and the Bill of Rights to overturn state action considered prejudicial or restrictive. It was during this period that the Fourteenth Amendment finally began to fulfill its purpose, providing a shield to those who were victims of their own state governments.

In the last few years, the attitude toward the federal government has changed. People today are reviving some of the fears early Americans had toward the central government. States are reaffirming their power in many matters, such as welfare reform. During this time, the Supreme Court has also become more conservative and has restricted some of the provisions of earlier decisions. Thus the fascinating process that keeps our Constitution and Bill of Rights living, breathing instruments continues to reshape our understanding of what it means to be an American.

6 The Fifth Amendment: Freedom from Self-Incrimination

The Fifth Amendment protection most people are familiar with is the right of a person to refuse to incriminate, or provide evidence against, himself or herself. It has become a common part of our language. Anyone who has ever seen a cops and robbers movie or television show is familiar with the phrase "take the Fifth," meaning to refuse to testify. Similarly, the standard method of invoking the right on the stand, "I refuse to answer on the grounds that it might tend to incriminate me," is as familiar as the Miranda warning (discussed later in this chapter) that police officers must read to people they arrest. Yet what exactly is the privilege invoked when a person uses his or her Fifth Amendment right? And why did the founders feel it was so necessary that they included it in the Bill of Rights?

Although to us today it may seem a matter of common sense that no person should have to help convict himself or herself, this was almost never the case in the past. People familiar with British and American law (such as the

46

founders) were familiar with the infamous English Star Chamber courts of the sixteenth and seventeenth centuries. Persons could be brought before these courts without being told what they were being charged with and made to swear to answer any questions put to them under pain of imprisonment or torture. Also, they could be compelled to be a witness against themselves—in other words, to destroy any defense they might make by admitting to the charge of which they were accused.

The Star Chambers were hateful to anyone who loved liberty, and their abuses were long remembered by people raised within the Anglo-American justice system. (Indeed, although outlawed in England in 1641, the abuses perpetuated by the Star Chambers inspired several of the protections to the accused found in the Bill of Rights.) Within the English legal system, the freedom from self-incrimination became deeply ingrained and served as another source of British pride in the superiority of their system over the repressive systems of other nations. The colonists inherited this principle from their English forebears. Even under the strain of the Revolution, both acknowledged that no person should ever be forced to incriminate himself or herself.

After the Revolution, many states drafted bills of rights, including a protection from self-incrimination, to accompany their state constitutions; however, the protection often applied only to people accused of a crime. Even those that did include the protection often made it apply only to people accused of a crime. However, James Madison's Fifth Amendment contains no such restriction; anyone, not just someone accused of a crime, can use the Fifth Amendment to protect himself or herself.

The Nature of the Privilege

A person's Fifth Amendment rights are not automatic. They must be invoked by that person, or they are considered waived. And even if the privilege is claimed, a judge must decide if it is justified. Generally, this requires that there is a real danger of the person being convicted of a crime for what he or she says.

The privilege covers all evidence, including testimony, confessions, and physical evidence. A person is never required to give these up if the evidence can be used to convict him or her. Furthermore, the privilege gives any accused person the right to plead not guilty. The Supreme Court has determined that a person can begin using this privilege as soon as the police begin interrogating him or her.

"Taking the Fifth" may be done by people who are innocent as well as people who are guilty. The Court has repeatedly ruled that a person's use of his or her Fifth Amendment right cannot be considered as evidence of guilt by a jury.

The privilege applies only to the person who invokes it. It cannot be used to shield another person. It also does not include corporations, unions, or other organizations. Only the personal and private documents of a person are covered; if the person is in possession of public documents or the records of an organization, these items are not protected by privilege.

One of the most important protections of the Fifth Amendment is its protection from forced confessions and testimony. For this reason, the Supreme Court has found that states may not fire employees who refuse to testify about job-related activities. These employees likewise cannot be punished for invoking their Fifth Amendment privilege, and the Court has overturned convictions of employees who were convicted after giving in to pressure from their employers. It is very important to note, however, that people accused of crimes lose their Fifth Amendment privilege if they take the stand in their own defense.

Immunity

There are times when the government feels that it has an overwhelming interest in compelling a witness to testify, despite his or her use of the Fifth Amendment privilege. On other occasions, the state may wish to use the testimony of a person involved in a crime another person has been charged with—yet if the witness testifies, he or she will incriminate himself or herself. In response to situations such as these, prosecutors have developed a concept called immunity.

Simply put, immunity guarantees that any information a witness reveals will not be used to convict him or her. Problems have arisen, however, in deciding just how immune a person will be from conviction. Does immunity prevent the state from prosecuting the person at all for any crimes he or she admits to? Can the state use any evidence that the person reveals? These are important considerations because the government often uses immunity to compel, or force, a person to testify. By removing the danger of prosecution, the government can ask the court to make the person speak because his or her Fifth Amendment privilege no longer applies.

Immunity must be provided for by law. It is not a power of the courts and can be granted only by Congress or a state legislature. The early immunity laws prevented the government from prosecuting a person for any crime he or she provided evidence for while testifying. Later laws, however, attempted to allow the indirect use of such testimony.

In 1892, the Supreme Court, in *Counselman v. Hitchcock,* ruled that this limited immunity was insufficient protection of a person's freedom from self-incrimination. At this time, the federal government was attempting to combat corruption in the railroad industry. Concerned that witnesses would not come forward unless some immunity was granted, Congress allowed a "transactional" immunity, which protects a person not only from the use of testimony as evidence, but prosecution from any criminal "transactions" revealed in his or her testimony.

This type of immunity was upheld in 1896 by the Court's decision in *Brown v. Walker.* This case also established the important principles that the privilege could not be used merely to shield others, nor could it be used to protect a person's reputation. The privilege applied only to conviction for crimes—thus, if a person was granted immunity from prosecution of any crimes his or her testimony was evidence of, that person could not assert the Fifth Amendment privilege. This was upheld again in *Ullmann v. United States* (1956). There, the Court held that a person who had been granted immunity against prosecution as a communist could not still assert his or her Fifth Amendment privilege even though he or she would suffer socially—by perhaps losing a job or being criticized by the public—by testifying about his or her activities as a member of the Communist Party.

The Organized Crime Control Act of 1970 allowed prosecutors to convict criminals who had hoped for immunity in exchange for their testimony. The photo above shows mobster Joseph Barboza testifying before a House committee in 1972.

The question of immunity was revisited with the passage of the Organized Crime Control Act of 1970. This act provided for more limited "use" immunity where a person could still be prosecuted for crimes that he or she implicated himself or herself in during testimony, provided the evidence used to convict him or her was independent of that testimony. In other words, if the government could find evidence for the crime that did not stem directly from the individual's testimony, the government could convict the person of a crime mentioned in his or her testimony. This ruling allowed prosecutors to convict criminals—mostly members of organized crime—who had hoped to escape conviction for all their crimes by testifying about a select few. In *Kastigar v. United States* (1972), this type of immunity was upheld.

The Fifth Amendment and the States

It took until 1964 for the Supreme Court to rule that the Fifth Amendment applied to the states as well as the federal government. Various attempts were made to use the due process clause of the Fourteenth Amendment to make the Fifth Amendment applicable to the states, but the Court ruled in both *Twining v. New Jersey* (1908) and *Adamson v. California* (1947) that the privilege was not a part of due process.

To make matters more confusing, the Court had held in other rulings that the states could use testimony compelled under immunity by a federal court in state prosecution, and the federal courts could do likewise with compelled state testimony, making a hollow mockery of privilege.

In 1964, the Court overturned *Twining* with its decision in *Malloy v. Hogan*. William Malloy had been convicted of illegal gambling activities. He was then ordered to testify to a state investigation of the gambling activities of Hartford, Connecticut. He refused, claiming his Fifth Amendment rights, and was sentenced to jail for contempt of court. His appeal eventually reached the Supreme Court, which upheld it and ruled that the Fifth Amendment protection from self-incrimination did apply to the states. The same day that the decision in *Malloy* was announced, the Court also held, in *Murphy v. Waterfront Commission of New York*, that immunity granted under either federal or state authority protects a person from both federal and state prosecution. The days when state or federal governments could use immunity to gather evidence to prosecute a person under the other jurisdiction were over.

Voluntary and Involuntary Confessions

A confession is extremely valuable in prosecuting a crime. A confession can be used against a person even if the person later maintains his or her innocence. However, a person who is threatened or tortured may confess to a crime that he or she did not commit, just to avoid the threat or torture. Thus, the federal courts have for a long time ruled that only a voluntary confession may be admissible as evidence. The question then is, when does a confession become involuntary? At what point does the government put so much pressure on a person that his or her confession must be considered involuntary?

By 1896, the Court had held that a confession must be made without any compulsion or inducement—in other words, the government could not threaten or promise to reward a person in order to get that person to confess. This test had to be applied to any confession, for the circumstances in which each confession was made could have an enormous influence on the state of mind of the person who confessed.

The Supreme Court, in the twentieth century, ruled that excessive delay in charging a person with a crime can make any confession illegal and inadmissible. Two landmark cases, both involving the federal court system, made this thinking clear.

The first case was *McNabb v. United States* (1943). In this case, several men had been convicted of killing a federal revenue agent, a person charged with the collection of certain taxes. The key piece of evidence against the men was statements they had made that incriminated them. These statements, however, had been made after three days of questioning, without the presence of their lawyers and without a crime having been formally charged against them. The Supreme Court overturned the convictions, not on the basis of the Fifth Amendment, but rather on federal criminal procedure laws and its power to oversee the working of the federal courts.

The second case, *Mallory v. United States* (1957), proved to be extremely controversial. In this case, the Court overturned the conviction and death sentence of a man who had confessed to rape. The confession, however, had come during a more than eighteen-hour delay between his arrest and his arraignment (the appearance before a judge where a person accused of a crime pleads either guilty or not guilty). Furthermore, when first arrested, he had strongly denied his guilt. The Court found his detention to be excessive and the confession to have been coerced. The outcry over this case led to Congress writing laws that allowed the use of some confessions obtained during a delay between arrest and arraignment.

In federal cases, the guiding principle behind whether or not a confession was voluntary or not was the Fifth Amendment. However, even before the *Mallory* ruling incorporated the Fifth Amendment against the states, the Supreme Court had used the Fourteenth Amendment to rule that certain confessions were in fact involuntary and therefore inadmissible.

The Supreme Court's decision in *Mallory v. United States* determined that forced confessions violated a suspect's Fifth Amendment rights.

In *Brown v. Mississippi* (1936), the Court overturned the convictions of three black men who had been convicted of murder on the basis of their confessions. The police had obtained these confessions by beating and whipping the men, and then telling them that they would be beaten further if they changed their stories. During the trial, the men testified that they had been beaten and that their confessions were false. After their convictions, they appealed to the Supreme Court. The state of Mississippi argued that the confessions should be considered valid because the Fifth Amendment did not apply to state trials.

However, the Supreme Court ruled that the Fourteenth Amendment's due process clause did not allow for the torture of people accused of a crime. This was the first case in which torture was ruled to make a confession illegal.

In a later case, *Chambers v. Florida* (1940), the Court held that the pressure used against an accused person need not be physical to force a confession. In *Chambers*, four black men were convicted of murder, again on the basis of their confessions. They had been held without any access to the outside world and questioned repeatedly over several days, until each one, after denying his guilt over that time, finally broke down and confessed. Again, the Court used the due process clause of the Fourteenth Amendment to overturn the convictions, clearly finding that the methods used by the police violated any understanding of fairness.

After the *Malloy* case, of course, the Fifth Amendment also applied to the states, meaning confessions could be thrown out because they violated a person's freedom from self-incrimination. However, the most important principle the Supreme Court observed was that a confession was so damaging that it must be made without any force being applied to the person who made it. Justice Felix Frankfurter noted, in *Rogers v. Richmond* (1961):

> *Our decisions have made clear . . . that convictions following the admission into evidence of confessions which are involuntary . . . cannot stand. This is so not because such confessions are unlikely to be true but because the methods used to extract them offend. . . .*

In other words, for a confession to be admissible, it was not important whether or not it was true, but whether it was freely given. The greater injustice is to force someone to confess to a crime, whether or not he or she has actually committed it.

The Right to Counsel and Confessions

As previously noted, the Fifth and Sixth Amendments are very closely linked, and each reinforces the rights of the other. One of the most important rights of the Sixth Amendment is the right of an accused person to have a lawyer, or counsel, to assist in his or her defense. Starting in the 1960s, the Supreme Court, in a reversal of earlier rulings, decided that the Fifth Amendment's protection from self-incrimination required that a person must be allowed to have a lawyer present during questioning. More important, it ruled that once a suspect asks for a lawyer, the police must stop questioning him or her until the lawyer is provided. Any confession that occurred without a lawyer present after the suspect had asked for one would be inadmissible.

The case that established the above procedure, *Escobedo v. Illinois* (1964), was controversial enough; but a later case, *Miranda v. Arizona* (1966), provoked a firestorm of criticism from law enforcement workers because of its requirement that a suspect have all of his or her rights explained and be warned of the consequences of not using these rights. The *Miranda* decision, however, has never been overturned, and it forever changed the face of law enforcement in the United States.

Escobedo v. Illinois

Danny Escobedo was arrested by police with a legal warrant at 2:30 in the morning and questioned about a murder for which he was a suspect. He denied his guilt, and his lawyer managed to get him released. Several days later, the police again arrested him and began to question him. Escobedo asked to consult with his lawyer, but the police refused to allow him to do so, even though his lawyer had arrived at the police station shortly after Danny's arrest. The police continued to question him, and during this time he made several admissions that implicated him in the murder. At no time did the police tell him that he had the right to remain silent and refuse to answer any questions. Escobedo was later convicted of murder.

The Supreme Court overturned his conviction, agreeing with Escobedo's claim that he had been denied his Sixth Amendment right to counsel because the police had not told him—as his lawyer certainly would have—of his right to remain silent. The case was also related to the 1963 decision in *Gideon v. Wainwright* (see chapter 9), which required that any person being tried for a serious crime must be allowed to have a lawyer present to assist in his or her defense. To the thinking of the majority of the Court, the protection of counsel would be meaningless if a suspect was not allowed the assistance of a lawyer to prevent him or her from making a confession while being questioned by police.

The vote on *Escobedo* was 5-4, indicating how divided the Court was on this issue. The major implication of the case was that the Court's historic test for the admissibility of a confession, that it be voluntary, no longer applied. If a

The landmark Supreme Court case *Miranda v. Arizona* helped create guidelines for legal interrogation. The photo above shows Ernesto Miranda (right) leaving court with his lawyer.

suspect made a voluntary confession without the presence of his or her lawyer, it might still be ruled inadmissible. However, the next landmark case, *Miranda v. Arizona,* helped to create guidelines as to whether or not an interrogation was legal.

Miranda v. Arizona

Ernesto Miranda had been convicted for kidnapping and rape in Arizona. The case against him relied on statements he had made during his interrogation by the police, who never informed him that he could remain silent or consult an attorney. Again, by a 5-4 vote, the Supreme Court overturned his conviction for clearly violating the principles set out in *Escobedo.* Chief Justice Earl Warren, however, went further, holding that in order for an interrogation to be legal and its results admissible,

> *the following measures are required. He [the suspect] must be warned prior to any questioning that he has the right to remain silent, that anything he says can be used against him in a court of law, that he has the right to the presence of an attorney, and that if he cannot afford an attorney one will be appointed for him prior to any questioning if he so desires.*

This is the origin of the famous Miranda warnings that are familiar to anyone who has watched a television show or movie about the police. In other words, the Court held that any questioning that began after the suspect had been informed of his or her rights would be legal. It further held that a suspect could waive, or give up, these rights if he or she chose to, provided that the decision was made "voluntarily, knowingly, and intelligently." This allowed voluntary confessions made without the presence of counsel admissible, provided the person making the confession understood the rights he or she was giving up.

Miranda proved to be even more controversial than *Escobedo,* since it forced police departments all across the country to adopt new rules. Also, since arrests made without the reading of Miranda warnings could result in inadmissible evidence, many felt that the decision was "soft on criminals." The Court had reduced some of the effects of *Miranda* by ruling that it applied only to

DEFENDANT	LOCATION

SPECIFIC WARNING REGARDING INTERROGATIONS

1. You have the right to remain silent.

2. Anything you say can and will be used against you in a court of law.

3. You have the right to talk to a lawyer and have him present with you while you are being questioned.

4. If you cannot afford to hire a lawyer one will be appointed to represent you before any questioning, if you wish one.

SIGNATURE OF DEFENDANT	DATE
WITNESS	TIME

☐ REFUSED SIGNATURE   SAN FRANCISCO POLICE DEPARTMENT   PR.9.1.4

The *Miranda* case forced police departments to adopt new rules. This card detailing the Miranda warnings was presented to suspects by the San Francisco Police Department in the 1960s.

cases that went to trial after the decision; in other words, it could not be used to make a confession that occurred before the *Miranda* decision inadmissible. Still, the charges by law enforcement professionals and even members of Congress that the Supreme Court was keeping the police and the government from putting guilty people in jail had effects not only on a presidential election but on the makeup of the Court itself. Richard Nixon made promises during his successful 1968 campaign to reestablish "law and order" and to appoint justices to the Supreme Court who would be less protective of criminal suspects. Consequently, between 1969 and 1971, President Nixon nominated three more conservative justices to the Court, including a new chief justice, Warren Burger.

The Supreme Court has been more conservative since the *Miranda* decision, especially under Chief Justice William Rehnquist.

Ironically, Ernesto Miranda was retried by Arizona and convicted on the testimony of his common-law wife. He was paroled in 1972 and had several more run-ins with the police until he was stabbed to death in 1976. His attacker was read his Miranda warning when he was arrested.

Continuing Controversies

The Supreme Court, under the leadership of Chief Justice Warren Burger (who served as chief justice from 1969 to 1986) and especially Chief Justice William Rehnquist (named chief justice in 1986), has been more conservative since the *Miranda* decision. Several important cases ruled on in the 1950s and 1960s have had their impacts diminished, although they have not been overturned.

In 1991, for example, the Court held in *Arizona v. Fulminante* that a coerced confession did not necessarily require a new trial if the rest of the evidence was so strong that the person would have been convicted anyway. This ruling overturned twenty-four years of precedent that held that a forced confession always required a new trial.

The controversial *Miranda* decision has likewise never been overturned, but several cases and laws have made it possible to sometimes obtain information without the Miranda warnings having been given. In 1968, for example, Congress wrote laws that allowed federal judges to use confessions whenever they felt they had been made voluntarily. This affected only federal trials, however; *Miranda* remained in effect in the states.

Since 1966, the Court has also held that on occasion the public's right to safety was greater than a suspect's right to avoid incriminating himself or herself. The Court has also held that the request for a lawyer must be clearly a request for a lawyer and not a vague statement. If the suspect does not make a clear request, the police are not required to ask him or her to be more clear.

Even with these modifications, by enforcing these principles, the Supreme Court has continues to make the U.S. system of justice as fair as possible. A free society cannot operate without the practices the Fifth Amendment secures; the Supreme Court has merely guaranteed that no person accused of a crime need to fear that he or she will be forced to become his or her own worst witness.

7 The Fifth Amendment: Protection from Double Jeopardy

Double jeopardy refers to the principle, as stated in the Fifth Amendment, that no person can be twice put in danger of losing his or her life, liberty, or property. This idea is crucial to protecting a person from unjust and excessive prosecution. Without it, the government could repeatedly try a person who had been found not guilty until it got a conviction. However, determining whether or not a person has in fact been put into "jeopardy" for a given offense has turned out to be one of the most complex and difficult subjects the Court has ever addressed.

Double jeopardy prevents a person from being tried more than once for the same crime by the same government. As we shall see, it does not prevent a person from being tried by different governing bodies—two states, for example, or the state and federal government—when the actions are crimes under more than one jurisdiction.

There are two very important aspects of double jeopardy that always apply. The first is that the government

65

may not appeal an acquittal: If a jury finds a person not guilty, the state may not retry him or her again for that matter, even if that person is in fact guilty. The second is that a person may waive his or her freedom from double jeopardy in order to be retried for the same offense. This can happen if, for example, a judge decides that because of mistakes in the original trial, the person is entitled to a second trial. If a person chooses this option, however, he or she must give up protection from double jeopardy.

Of critical importance in deciding whether or not a person is protected from prosecution by his or her freedom from double jeopardy is when he or she is actually in jeopardy; that is, at what point is the accused in danger of being punished? The Supreme Court has decided that jeopardy "attaches" (that is, makes it possible to avoid further prosecution for this offense under the double jeopardy protection) as soon as a jury is sworn in or the first piece of evidence is presented or witness is sworn in (if the case does not have a jury). Once this has happened, only the failure of a jury to reach a verdict, or certain exceptional kinds of mistrial, can keep jeopardy from attaching.

Incorporation of Double Jeopardy

Like all the rights included in the Bill of Rights, the double jeopardy protection did not initially apply to the states. It was not until the 1960s that a more liberal Court overturned previous decisions and made the protection apply to the states as well as the federal government. Two cases in particular set the limits on the double jeopardy clause: *Palko v. Connecticut* (1937) and *Benton v. Maryland* (1969).

In *Palko,* the Court found that the Fourteenth Amendment did not extend the protection of double jeopardy to the states. Frank Palko had been convicted of second-degree murder, although the state had indicted him for first-degree murder as well. The state, however, appealed the decision, claiming legal errors had been made. A new trial was ordered, and this second trial resulted in a conviction for first-degree murder and the death penalty. Palko appealed to the Supreme Court, which allowed his conviction to stand, finding that retrying a case because of legal error did not violate the double jeopardy clause.

Federal standards for double jeopardy protection were much stronger, as the curious case of *Green v. United States* (1957) demonstrates. Evrett Green was charged with murder and arson in the death of his neighbor. Because the crime occurred in the District of Columbia, he was tried by the federal courts. At his trial, the judge informed the jury that it must decide if Green was guilty of arson, murder in the first degree, or murder in the second degree. This was important because under the laws of the District of Columbia, a person found guilty of first-degree murder automatically received the death penalty. The jury found Green guilty of arson and second-degree murder. Green was sentenced to prison, but his lawyers found legal mistakes in his trial that would allow him to receive a new trial. To do so, however, he had to waive his protection from double jeopardy in the crimes of which he had been convicted. Green decided to proceed with the second trial, and this time was found guilty of first-degree murder and sentenced to death.

Green appealed to the Supreme Court, claiming that his protection from double jeopardy was violated by giving him the death penalty when, at his first trial, the jury had not found him guilty of first-degree murder. He claimed that since it had had the chance to convict him of first-degree murder, and had not done so, it was the same thing as acquitting him of first-degree murder—in which case, the Fifth Amendment would prevent the state from trying him again. The Court agreed and overturned his first-degree murder conviction. However, under the rules set forth in *Palko,* this ruling did not include the states, even though there were many similarities between the two cases.

It was not until 1969, in *Benton v. Maryland,* that the Court finally overturned *Palko* and extended the protection of the double jeopardy clause to the states. John Dalmer Benton had been tried for larceny and burglary in Maryland. A jury convicted him of burglary but acquitted him of larceny. Because of errors made during jury selection, a new trial was ordered, which found him guilty of both charges, despite his lawyers' attempts to get the larceny charge thrown out because of double jeopardy. The Supreme Court heard his appeal and ruled that the federal guidelines of *Green v. United States* should also apply to the states. Justice Thurgood Marshall, noting that they were merely "recognizing the inevitable," pointed out that the recent decisions of the Court had destroyed the notion that the Fourteenth Amendment provided only a "watered-down" version of the Bill of Rights and continued the process of giving all citizens its protections.

In 1981, in *Bullington v. Missouri,* the Court applied the same ruling it had come to in *Green* to the states, ruling that the state should not get a chance to seek the death penalty in a new trial when a jury had refused to impose it in the original trial.

Separate Sovereignty

As noted previously, the double jeopardy protection does not prevent multiple trials for the same act, provided that a different government prosecutes each trial separately and under its own laws. The most common way this can occur is when both the federal government and a state try a person for an act that is against both federal and state laws. There are many such acts.

The principle of "separate sovereignty" (sovereignty means a separate or independent government) was established in 1922 in the case of *United States v. Lanza* and has never been overturned. The defendant in the case, Vito Lanza, had been found guilty of violating Washington State's prohibition law (a law that enforced the famous Eighteenth Amendment, which banned the sale and possession of alcoholic beverages in the United States) and then was tried for violating the federal prohibition law. He appealed on the grounds that his conviction by the state should give him double jeopardy protection from prosecution for a federal crime that was, after all, the same act. Chief Justice (and former president) William Howard Taft ruled against him, finding that an offense that was against the law of two different governments could be prosecuted by both of them. (His ruling also relied on the fact that the Fifth Amendment did not apply to the states, but this fact, since overturned, has not changed the basic doctrine of separate sovereignty.)

One notable use of separate sovereignty was the federal civil rights violation case against Los Angeles police sergeant Stacy Koon and three other officers involved in the beating of Rodney King.

The separate sovereignty rule even allows for a state to attempt to convict a person who has been previously acquitted by a federal court. In *Bartkus v. Illinois* (1959), Alphonse Bartkus, who had been tried and acquitted by a federal court for bank robbery, was then tried by an Illinois court and found guilty. His appeal, on the grounds of double jeopardy, was denied, again under the principle of separate sovereignty. However, the Justice Department soon thereafter announced a policy of not pursuing a federal trial following a state trial for a crime involving the same act unless there was a "compelling" reason to do so.

Separate sovereignty, though, applies only to the states and the federal government, or a state and another state. In *Waller v. Florida* (1970), the Court ruled that a city government was not separate enough from the government of the state it was in to avoid the double jeopardy clause.

Although the principle of separate sovereignty may seem unfair at first glance, it has in fact been used on several occasions to right an injustice. During the 1960s, many crimes by whites against blacks in the South that resulted in acquittals by prejudiced juries were then successfully prosecuted by the federal government— usually because crimes such as murder or assault deprived the victim of his or her federal civil rights. One notable use of separate sovereignty was the 1992 trial of the policemen accused of beating Rodney King in Los Angeles. After a Los Angeles jury had acquitted the officers, federal charges were brought against two of them, which resulted in their convictions.

Multiple Offenses

How does double jeopardy apply when one act can constitute several different crimes? This is one of the most difficult areas of double jeopardy law. One difficulty is that many actions do violate several laws because of the overlapping nature of the criminal code. For example, if two people plan to kill someone, and they then shoot him to death, they can be charged with murder, conspiracy to commit murder, and if they do not have permits for their guns, illegal possession of weapons.

Two different interpretations of how the Court should apply the double jeopardy protection reflect the changing attitude of the Court before and after the landmark *Benton* decision. In the first case, *Hoag v. New Jersey* (1958), the Court ruled that a state could prosecute a person multiple times for related crimes that stemmed from the same act. Hoag had been indicted for the robbery of five people in a New Jersey bar. At his first trial, however, he was tried only for robbing three of them. He was acquitted, and the state then prosecuted him for the robbery of a fourth person. His appeal to the Supreme Court was denied, as the majority felt that he was not being subjected to repeated prosecution for the same offense.

In a similar case in 1970, however, *Ashe v. Swenson,* the Court reversed this thinking in the light of the expanded Fifth Amendment protections granted by the *Benton* ruling. The case involved the robbery of a group of six poker players by three or four masked men. Ashe was indicted as one of the robbers and tried for the crime of robbing one of the poker players. He was acquitted in that case, and the state then tried and convicted him for robbing another of the poker players. The Court overturned this conviction. Had Ashe been convicted in the first trial, the state would have been free to try him for robbing each of the other five poker players; but once the first jury had acquitted him, no further prosecution stemming from the original crime could be brought against him.

The Brief History of the Same Conduct Rule

In the 1990 case *Grady v. Corbin*, a new addition to the double jeopardy protection was found to exist by the Court. In *Grady*, a defendant had pleaded guilty to driving while intoxicated and failing to keep on the right side of the road. Unbeknownst to the judge who accepted his plea, the driver had allegedly caused an accident that resulted in the death of another driver. Later, the person was indicted for reckless manslaughter and criminally negligent homicide.

The suspect appealed these indictments to the Supreme Court, which, in a 5-4 decision, ruled that jeopardy had attached once he had pleaded guilty to the lesser crimes. This was because the acts involved in the lesser crimes— essentially, driving while drunk and being on the wrong side of the road—were the same as the acts involved in the greater crime; they stemmed from the "same conduct."

This new protection lasted just three years. In 1993, in *United States v. Dixon*, the Court reversed the earlier decision. A defendant who had been placed under a court order not to approach his wife was convicted of violating that court order in an incident where he beat her and kicked her down the basement stairs. He was then indicted for assaulting her. The Court's decision said that although he could not be indicted for simple assault, he could be indicted for other crimes, such as assault with the intention to kill, that the earlier jury had not heard. The basis for overturning the original decision was its "lack of constitutional roots" and the fact that it had proved to be "unstable in application." It should also be noted, however, that this decision was reached by the same vote as the previous one, 5-4, and that between the two cases two of the justices who had voted in the first case had been replaced by new justices, one of whom voted to overturn *Grady.*

Other Aspects of Double Jeopardy Protection

In the 1994 case of *Montana Department of Revenue v. Kurth Ranch,* the Supreme Court used the double jeopardy protection to strike down a state tax on illegal drugs. Because the state tried to collect this money from people convicted of drug offenses, and because the taxes were so high, the Court decided that the people being taxed were essentially being punished twice for the same crime, and it applied the double jeopardy protection.

The Court has also ruled (based on the decisions that kept the death penalty from being imposed in a second trial if it was not imposed in the first trial) that the penalties a judge imposes on a person convicted in his or her

The double jeopardy protection applies only to criminal prosecution. As in the famous case of O.J. Simpson, a civil suit can be filed against a person acquitted of criminal charges.

second trial cannot be worse than the penalties the person received in his or her first trial. However, a jury can still impose higher penalties.

One final note: The double jeopardy protection applies only to criminal prosecution. Even if a person is acquitted of a crime, he or she can still be sued for "damages" in civil court, where the burden of proof is much lower than in criminal court. The most famous recent example of this rule is the civil suit brought against O.J. Simpson by the families of the two people he was acquitted of murdering.

8 Due Process and Jury Trials: Guarantees of Fairness

The previous chapters have mentioned the concept of due process, especially the due process clause of the Fourteenth Amendment, which has been used to make the rights guaranteed by the Bill of Rights apply to the states as well as the federal government—the process known as incorporation. But what exactly does due process mean?

Due process is a guarantee of fairness. In other words, the government must follow established rules (known as procedures) in the accusation, indictment, trial, and sentencing of people accused of a crime. The Fifth and Fourteenth Amendments also make clear that these rules must be followed the same way for all persons accused of crimes. It is clearly unfair to follow the rules for one group of people and ignore them or use a different set of rules for another group of people. Sadly, this was the case in the United States for many years: White men were given preferential treatment over African Americans, women, Native Americans, and immigrants. For much of the first 100 years that the Fourteenth Amendment was part of the Constitution, its requirements that all U.S. citizens receive both due process and the equal protection of the law were ignored or stripped of any real meaning. Only during the latter part of the twentieth century did the Supreme Court begin to change its previous rulings and grant all people the full bounty of freedom that the Fourteenth Amendment promised.

Deciding what constitutes due process, however, is one of the most complex issues any court can be called upon to decide. There is no single or set answer for what due process requires. However, the Fifth, Sixth, and Fourteenth Amendments have certain "bedrock" rights that cannot be taken away or restricted without violating due process. Another test used by the Supreme Court is the idea of "fundamental fairness," the idea that a trial must be conducted in such a way that no side has an unfair advantage. The fundamental fairness rule was used in the early part of the twentieth century to protect people accused of crimes even before the "incorporation" of the Bill of Rights.

Indictments

The Fifth Amendment requires that an indictment by a grand jury is required in order to try a person accused of a capital or "infamous" crime. As simple as this concept sounds, it is very complex in practice.

First, an indictment is a formal, written statement charging a person with a crime. In federal cases, the indictment must be given by a special jury called a grand jury. The grand jury is a group of between twelve and twenty-three citizens who hear evidence presented by the government and determine whether or not there is enough "probable cause" that a person has committed the crime the government accuses him or her of to try that person. Probable cause simply means that the juries believe the charge is likely true.

Grand juries have a very long tradition in Anglo-American law; they have been in existence since the thirteenth century and originally decided both if a case should be tried and then if the person was guilty. These functions were later separated. The purpose of a grand jury is to keep the government from using its ability to charge people with crimes oppressively; the idea is the same as that of using a regular (petit) jury during a trial—that if the government must convince a group of citizens that a person has committed a crime, then there is less chance that innocent people will be victimized by the government. A grand jury differs from a petit jury in a number of respects. First, it usually has more than twelve people on it. Second, in most grand jury proceedings, the jury does not have to vote unanimously to grant an indictment; only a majority of the jurors need to agree with the state. Finally, many of the normal rules of evidence do not apply to grand jury proceedings. It may consider evidence that would not be admissible at trial to determine whether or not probable cause exists.

The Fifth Amendment and federal law require a grand jury indictment for all capital cases and other infamous crimes. A capital case is one that requires the death penalty; the Supreme Court has defined an infamous crime as any that would result in a sentence for a period longer than six months in a federal prison. Crimes that do not result in either of these two provisions do not require an indictment.

This part of the Fifth Amendment has never been held to apply to the states; it was decided in the 1884 case *Hurtado v. California* that there is no constitutional requirement for a state to have a grand jury system, and approximately half of them do not. The *Hurtado* decision requires only "information" that there is probable cause. However, the Sixth Amendment requires that a person accused of a crime be informed of the charges against him or her, and the Supreme Court has held that this applies to the states as well.

The most basic part of this Sixth Amendment protection is that a person held by the police must be told what he or she is accused of doing. The police cannot simply keep a person in custody without giving a reason. However, larger issues raised by this Sixth Amendment protection have caused the Supreme Court to strike down laws in some cases.

This is because the Court has held that a law must be clear in order for it to be legal. That is, a person must be able to understand exactly what that law makes a criminal act. Laws that are too vague can be overturned. In general, the Court demands that a law must be clear in precisely what action is illegal, although there have been cases where a vaguely worded law has been allowed to stand because other courts have made clear what the law means in action.

A related right of the accused found in the original Constitution, not in the Bill of Rights, is the protection from *ex post facto* laws. Latin for "after the fact," an *ex post facto* law is one that makes an action illegal that was not illegal

Trial by jury has long been a feature of English law. Some people
believe that it was instituted during the reign of King Alfred the Great.

when the action occurred. However, the Court has held since the 1798 decision in *Calder v. Bull* that a law may also be considered an *ex post facto* law if it does any of the following: makes a crime more serious than when it was originally committed; changes the punishment for a crime, making it greater than when it was committed; or changes the rules of evidence, making it easier to bring damaging evidence or testimony against a person than when the crime was committed. These rules have never been overturned. A state or the federal government may still change its laws to make some crimes more serious (for example, the changes in the drug laws that occurred in the 1980s), but these changes cannot be applied retroactively, in other words, made to work against people who were arrested under the old laws.

Trial by Jury

So important did the framers believe trial by jury to be that it was included not once, but twice in the Constitution: first in Article III of the original Constitution, and then in the Sixth Amendment. The Seventh Amendment also guarantees trial by jury for civil cases involving amounts greater than $20.

Trial juries, like grand juries, have a very long history in British and American law. No one is sure when they became a feature of English law; some believe they were created during the reign of King Alfred the Great (849–899), while others feel they were a result of the Norman conquest of England in 1066. By the beginning of the thirteenth century, however, they were an established tradition, and the two types of juries, the grand juries, which decided if a crime had occurred, and the petit juries, which decided if the person being tried was in fact either guilty of the crime or not guilty, had been separated from one another.

In the English system, a jury usually consisted of twelve people, and the federal government adopted this rule for all criminal trials. In 1900, however, the Supreme Court ruled in *Maxwell v. Dow* that a state could use an eight-person jury. This decision also stated that, as with most of the rest of the Bill of Rights, the Sixth Amendment did not apply to the states, even under the Fourteenth Amendment.

The Supreme Court has held that a person may in fact waive his or her right to a jury trial, such as when he or she accepts a plea bargain. A person may also ask to have his or her case decided only by a judge, although the judge does not have to grant this request.

The Sixth Amendment right to trial by jury was one of the last rights to be incorporated against the states. It was not until 1968, in *Duncan v. Louisiana,* that the Court finally decided that due process required that the states allow a jury trial in all cases where federal guidelines required one.

However, this decision immediately conflicted with the previous case of *Maxwell v. Dow* because, while the federal government required juries of twelve people, the states were allowed to have fewer than that. Did the *Duncan* ruling therefore overturn the *Maxwell* decision?

In the 1970 case *Williams v. Florida,* the Court decided that it did not. A Florida law that provided only six-person juries except in capital cases was ruled to be constitutional, under the thinking that the framers of the Constitution had not anywhere specified the size of a jury, and that since

Florida law required that the jury decision be unanimous, the six-person jury was constitutional.

The 1972 case *Apodaca v. Oregon*, however, ruled that a jury decision need not be unanimous, upholding the conviction of Robert Apodaca for burglary, larceny, and assault with a deadly weapon by a 10-2 vote in the jury, which was the minimum margin that Oregon law required. A related case, *Johnson v. Louisiana,* allowed a 9-3 vote to stand.

The final piece in this puzzle was added in the 1979 case of *Burch v. Louisiana.* The question before the Court was, Could a jury of fewer than twelve people convict without a unanimous vote? The answer was no. Following the logic of the *Williams* decision, the Court found that in a jury as small as six people, a unanimous vote was necessary to preserve due process and ensure a fair trial. In the meanwhile, the Court had set six people as the smallest possible jury size in the 1978 case of *Ballew v. Georgia,* overturning a Georgia law that allowed five-person juries. Although Justice Lewis Powell noted that the line between five- and six-person juries was "hard to draw," such a line needed to be drawn in order to preserve the principle of a fair trial.

Getting a Fair Trial: Who Should Be on a Jury?

Central to the idea of having a fair trial is that the jury must be impartial: The language of the Sixth Amendment demands it. Long before the Sixth Amendment was held to apply to the states, however, the Supreme Court had acted against juries that were obviously unfairly constructed. The most common reason for this was lack of minorities on the jury.

One of the Court's earliest statements on this principle was the 1880 case *Strauder v. West Virginia*. Using the equal protection clause of the Fourteenth Amendment as its guide, the Court overturned the conviction of a black man because the laws of West Virginia did not allow blacks to serve on a jury. However, the Court later made clear that there was no requirement for blacks to appear on a jury, just that equal protection demanded that they not be excluded from serving.

Because of this, many states found ways to exclude blacks from juries without actually passing a law that did so, usually by making blacks meet requirements for jury service that were ignored for white people. However, in 1935 the Court took steps to correct this injustice in the second Scottsboro case, *Norris v. Alabama*. (The Scottsboro cases were named for the town in Alabama where they originally took place. The first Scottsboro case will be discussed in the next chapter.)

Clarence Norris, a black man, had been convicted by an all-white jury of the rape of a white woman. He appealed to the Supreme Court under the equal protection clause, pointing out how blacks were excluded from jury service. The Court agreed with him, deciding that the equal protection clause was a guarantee that had to be given in substance, and not merely paid lip service. The fact that no black person had apparently ever served on a jury in Scottsboro was enough for the Court to decide that equal protection had been denied. In 1937, the decision in *Patton*

Clarence Norris, a black man who had been convicted by an all-white jury, appealed to the Supreme Court under the equal protection clause in the second Scottsboro case.

v. *Mississippi* reinforced this ruling, overturning the conviction of a black man who had been indicted and convicted by an all-white jury.

A curious and infuriating example of how discrimination continued to keep blacks from serving on juries was the 1953 case of *Avery v. Georgia*. In order for a judge to pick possible jurors out of a pool of people qualified to serve, potential jurors had to write their names on pieces of paper, which were placed in a box. The judge then drew the required number of names from the box. However, white people wrote their names on white paper, while black people had to put their names on yellow paper. The Court struck down this system as unfair.

The 1964 decision in *Hernandez v. Texas* followed a similar logic. Pete Hernandez's conviction was overturned because the Court could find no person with a Latin-American name on any of the jury lists of the county he was convicted in for a period of twenty-five years prior to his conviction. Again, the Court found this kind of systematic discrimination to be blatantly unfair.

When deciding whether or not a person can serve on a jury, both the prosecuting attorney and the defense attorney may challenge the selection of that person. This means that they ask the judge not to allow that person to serve on this jury. The challenge may be for cause, meaning that either attorney believes the person cannot be impartial in the case being tried. When a potential juror is challenged for cause, the judge must then decide if he or she agrees with the attorney and will either exclude the person or allow him or her to serve on the jury. However, each attorney does have a limited number of peremptory challenges, which automatically exclude that person from serving on the jury; the judge has no say in the matter. (This process is called voir dire, from the old French words meaning "to speak the truth.")

In the 1986 case of *Batson v. Kentucky,* the Court found that it was unconstitutional for a peremptory challenge to be used to exclude a person if the only basis of the challenge was that person's race. The Kentucky state prosecutor, during jury selection for the trial of a black man, had used his peremptory challenges to eliminate all four black members of the pool that potential jurors were being chosen from. The Court, in later cases, expanded this ruling to include civil trials and to prevent defense attorneys from using their peremptory challenges in the same way.

As women have gained a greater say in American society, they, too, have become the source of Supreme Court decisions on whether a jury selection process that excludes them can be legal. In 1961, the Court was asked to decide the case of *Hoyt v. Florida,* which asked whether or not Florida's system of jury selection was legal. The Florida system included as potential jurors only those women who had signed a form indicating that they would like to be included on the jury list.

Gwendolyn Hoyt, who was accused of the murder of her husband, challenged this system under the equal protection clause. Following logic similar to that of the Scottsboro case, she contended that it was unfair for a jury that did not have women on it to try a case involving a woman. In a unanimous opinion, the Court upheld the Florida system. Women, the Court said, were still the "center of hearth and home" and needed to serve only when they felt a need to do so.

However, in 1975, the Court, perhaps finally realizing the changing nature of a woman's role in society, found no reason to continue to uphold the *Hoyt* decision. In *Taylor v. Louisiana,* the Court reversed the conviction of Billy Taylor, who contended that Louisiana's jury selection system, which was similar to Florida's, prevented him from receiving a fair trial. The Court agreed, finding that a system that excluded 53 percent of the population of the area the trial took place in could not possibly hold up under the equal protection clause. In the 1994 case *J.E.B v. Alabama,* the Court extended the ruling of the *Batson* case to include peremptory challenges made on the basis of gender.

Other Sixth Amendment Guarantees

Two other important parts of the Sixth Amendment also serve to protect people accused of a crime: the right to a speedy trial and the right to confront and cross-examine witnesses.

The right to a speedy trial is extremely important in order to preserve fairness. If it was not part of the Constitution, it might be possible for a person to be arrested and held for years before actually being tried. In a less extreme situation, the right to a speedy trial makes sure that the government does not continue to delay presenting its case in order to find more evidence, or make it impossible for some of the defendant's evidence or witnesses to be used. However, the protection applies only once a person has been arrested; so long as the government is acting in "good faith," reasonable delays in the process of investigating a crime are allowed, as are reasonable, good faith delays in the trial itself.

Until 1972, the federal government prosecuted cases under the belief that unless an accused person demanded a speedy trial, the person had essentially waived his or her right to one. This was changed after the Supreme Court's decision in *Barker v. Wingo,* which found that the Sixth Amendment right to a speedy trial could not be given up.

This part of the Sixth Amendment was not incorporated against the states until the 1967 case of *Klopfer v. North Carolina,* which ruled that a North Carolina law that allowed the government to delay the trial of someone who had been indicted for a crime for as long as the prosecutor wished was unconstitutional. The Court ruled that the right to a speedy trial was as fundamental to basic fairness as the rest of the Sixth Amendment and applicable even in the states.

The right to confront witnesses who testify against him or her is one of the most important rights a person accused of a crime can have. It prevents the government from using "secret" witnesses or unnamed accusers to denounce a person in court. It allows a person to know exactly who is speaking out against him or her and allows the preparation of an appropriate defense. A witness who is giving false testimony may find it too difficult to go on when forced to appear before the person he or she is accusing. And it prevents the use of hearsay by the government.

Hearsay means testimony delivered by someone who did not directly witness what he or she is describing but heard it from another person. Hearsay evidence is not admissible in court, and the Supreme Court has used the Sixth Amendment to prevent prosecutors from getting around its limitations.

The right to confront witnesses was incorporated against the states in the 1965 case *Pointer v. Texas*. In this case, the prosecution, without making any attempt to contact one witness, used a written transcript of that witness's testimony at trial. The Court overturned the conviction.

One of the most controversial aspects of this right is whether or not it applies to children who are the victims of abuse or rape. The Court has had to rule on whether a defendant's right to confront his or her accusers outweighs a child's right to not have to suffer even more emotional damage by being forced to face the person the child believes attacked him or her. An Iowa law that allowed a child to testify behind a screen was struck down by the Court in the 1988 case of *Coy v. Iowa.* The Court's opinion in that case was that a defendant had to be able to see his or her accusers face-to-face, and it noted that while this might damage a child who was the victim of an attack by the defendant, at the same time it would work against a child who was making a false or mistaken accusation.

However, two years later, in *Maryland v. Craig,* the Court seemed to reverse itself by allowing a child to testify over a closed-circuit television screen so that the child would never have to actually face the person he or she was accusing. In this case, the Court said that protecting the welfare of the child was more important than the witness's right of confrontation. In another decision that year, the Court also allowed the loosening of the hearsay rules in cases with child witnesses, provided that the hearsay testimony was checked for truthfulness.

All these Sixth Amendment rights protect an accused person by creating and safeguarding very specific procedures that try to make the trial as fair as possible. However, even if the rules provide for a fair trial, a person who does not know the rules, or understand how they work, might not make the best defense he or she could make simply out of ignorance. A person might not challenge damaging evidence that the government brings forth that it should not be allowed to use, or fail to use all of the rights the Constitution provides for him or her. The American legal system, which relies so much on precedent (rulings in similar cases that have been decided before), is very complicated and grows more so every year. Because of this, for any serious crime, a thorough knowledge of the law is absolutely essential to make a good defense.

The founders understood this when they wrote the Sixth Amendment, for another one of the rights it guarantees is the right to have a lawyer, or counsel, to assist in a person's defense. In a series of controversial decisions discussed in the next chapter, the Court was forced to decide just how important this right was and whether any trial conducted without the defendant being helped by a lawyer could be called fair.

9 The Sixth Amendment: The Right to Counsel

Having an effective lawyer to defend him or her is one of the most important rights an accused person has. Without such aid, a person can be nearly helpless. Because of this, both English and American law has long recognized that the government cannot prevent a person from having a lawyer with him or her at a trial. However, in the twentieth century, the Supreme Court began to consider the question of whether a person accused of a crime had a right to a lawyer even if he or she could not afford one.

History

English law for a long time recognized that a person should not, in principle, be deprived of counsel during a trial. However, this right did not extend to more serious crimes, such as treason or felonies, despite the fact that to our understanding, a person accused of such crimes would have the greatest need of a lawyer. The thinking of the English jurists seems to have been that such crimes would be prosecuted only when there was so much evidence that the person must be guilty; therefore, not only did the person not need a lawyer (being guilty) but the presence of a lawyer might actually result in a guilty person going free. However, an act of the British Parliament changed this in 1836.

The young American republic provided this right much earlier. Even before ratification of the Sixth Amendment, the Judiciary Act of 1789 gave defendants in federal cases the right to counsel no matter what the charges were, and most of the states had similar laws. Passage of the Sixth Amendment, of course, made this right constitutional in all federal cases; of course, it did not apply to the states until passage of the Fourteenth Amendment, and even then, as we shall see, the right was not extended to the people until the 1960s.

Federal law allowed for the appointment of a lawyer to people who could not afford one and to a defendant who requested it in any capital case as early as 1790. A few states also allowed a judge to appoint an attorney in capital cases. However, the Sixth Amendment provision guaranteeing the right to counsel was interpreted not as meaning that a defendant must be given counsel but only that the government could not keep him or her from hiring a lawyer. This was upheld by the Supreme Court's 1891 decision in *United States v. Van Duzee,* which also ruled that the 1790 law requiring a judge to appoint a lawyer in federal capital cases did not apply to lesser crimes.

The first Scottsboro case involved nine black men who were accused of raping two white girls. They were tried by a hostile, all-white jury and denied their right to effective counsel.

A Fundamental Right?

As we have seen, the due process clause of the Fourteenth Amendment has been used to gradually incorporate the rights guaranteed by the Bill of Rights against the states. While much of this work was done by the more liberal Supreme Courts of the 1960s, the Sixth Amendment right to counsel was first tested in the 1930s.

The first case in which the Supreme Court reversed a state conviction because the defendants were deprived of their right to counsel was the 1932 case *Powell v. Alabama*—known as the first Scottsboro case, for the town where the case was tried. (For a discussion of the important effects of the second Scottsboro case, *Norris v. Alabama,* see chapter 8.)

The first Scottsboro case involved the trial of nine black men who were accused of having raped two white girls while on a freight train. They were tried by an all-white jury in an area where the public was very hostile toward them. The nine men could not read and were not very well educated. Because of this, the trial judge appointed an attorney for them; on examination of the records, however, the Supreme Court justices could find no one who was specifically appointed to their defense. On the morning of the trial, a lawyer reluctantly came forward and offered to help the defendants with their case. The trial took less than a day to complete and resulted in the conviction of all the defendants.

The Supreme Court held that because of all these conditions, the defendants had been deprived of their right to effective counsel under the Sixth Amendment. The Court therefore reversed the convictions. This was the beginning of a momentary expansion of the Sixth Amendment rights.

In the case of *Johnson v. Zerbst,* the Court made two further important rulings. First, it overturned the 1891 *United States v. Van Duzee* decision, and it held that the defendant in a federal trial was guaranteed counsel, even if the person could not afford it, for any crime. The case itself involved a marine who was charged with passing counterfeit money. On the day of his trial, he showed up without an attorney present but told the judge that he was ready to continue anyway. The judge never mentioned his right to counsel or asked if he wanted a court-appointed attorney. Because of this, the Court reversed his conviction.

The other major result of this ruling was that in order for a defendant to give up the right to counsel in a federal trial, he or she had to understand the right not only to have an attorney but to ask the court to appoint one. In other words, before a defendant can give up, or waive, his or her right to counsel, that person must be competent—that is, fully aware of his or her situation and the charges he or she is accused of, and be able to aid in his or her defense—and make the choice intelligently, understanding both the consequences of giving up the right and the options available to him or her.

Much later, after the Court had determined that the Sixth Amendment did apply to the states, it ruled, in the 1975 case of *Faretta v. California,* that a defendant who was competent to stand trial could refuse even a court-appointed attorney and defend himself or herself. The Court held that while the Sixth Amendment guaranteed that a person must be offered legal representation, it did not make him or her have to accept such representation.

The Supreme Court soon made clear, however, that neither the *Powell* or *Johnson* decision applied the Sixth Amendment right to the states. In the case of the *Powell* ruling, the Court held that it was the specific circumstances of the case that had led to its decision, not any larger principle that extended the right. And the case of *Betts v. Brady* (1942) ruled that the states did not have to appoint a lawyer to a defendant who requested one, although the states themselves were free to write laws for themselves that required this. The crucial difference between the *Betts* and *Powell* cases was that the Court found that Smith Betts was of "ordinary intelligence and ability" and therefore not as handicapped as the Powell defendants. His lack of counsel did not hurt him in any serious way, according to the Court.

However, the *Betts* ruling left open the possibility that in any given case, there might be special circumstances like those of the first Scottsboro case that would allow the Supreme Court to rule that a defendant had been deprived of the right to counsel. Each case would have to be considered separately because the Court did not specify precisely what these "special circumstances" were. This situation was finally changed with the landmark decision that overturned *Betts*, *Gideon v. Wainwright*, one of the most important decisions ever handed down by the Court, a decision that changed forever the workings of the American justice system.

An Absolute Right

Clarence Earl Gideon was too poor to hire a lawyer when he was tried for the crime of breaking and entering a poolroom. At his trial, he requested that the judge appoint an attorney for him. The judge denied his request because under Florida law, the court was required to appoint a lawyer only in capital cases. Gideon then conducted his own defense: He gave an opening statement, put on witnesses to testify for him, and cross-examined the prosecution's witnesses. The jury in the case convicted him, and he was sentenced to five years in prison.

While in prison, Gideon taught himself about law and eventually sent a handwritten appeal to the Supreme Court, which agreed to hear his case in 1963. (Ironically, he was appointed an attorney to represent him before the Court.) The Court then decided to reverse his conviction. This overruled the *Betts* decision because Gideon clearly had been intelligent and capable enough to aid in his defense.

The *Gideon* decision meant that the states had to follow the rules established by the *Johnson v. Zerbst* case and provide an attorney to any person who asked for one. For the first time, the Court had ruled that the right to an attorney was an essential part of a fair trial.

In the 1972 case *Argersinger v. Hamlin*, the Supreme Court continued to expand the protection, ruling that a state had to provide an attorney in any case where there was the possibility of jail time, not just felonies or capital crimes. Again, this was an extension of the basic protection against loss of liberty without due process guaranteed by the Fifth Amendment and the Court's decisions that due process was not possible in a criminal case without the assistance of a lawyer.

The *Argersinger* ruling was later modified by rulings that it applied only when the trial judge wished to hold out the possibility of jail time. If the judge ruled that he or she

In the *Gideon* decision of 1963, the Supreme Court ruled that the right to an attorney was an essential part of a fair trial. Henry Fonda (above) portrayed Clarence Earl Gideon in a TV movie based on the case.

would not sentence a person to jail, even if the law allowed him or her to do so, the Supreme Court said that the states did not have to appoint defense counsel.

When Does a Person Have the Right to an Attorney?

Even before the *Gideon* decision, the Court had ruled that in cases where a person was entitled to ask for counsel, it must be given as early as was necessary to protect the rights of that person. In 1961, the Court ruled in *Hamilton v. Alabama* that in certain cases this was to be as early as arraignment. This was because certain types of pleas, such as insanity, could be made only at that time.

99

In 1964 and 1966, after the *Gideon* case, two other rulings of the Court extended this privilege to include questioning of a suspect by the police: *Escobedo v. Illinois* (1964) and *Miranda v. Arizona* (1966). Those cases continued to expand on the Court's contention, in *Gideon*, that a lawyer was necessary for the protection of an accused person's rights, even when he or she was being arrested or questioned by the police.

In 1967 the Court ruled on two related cases—*United States v. Wade* and *Gilbert v. California*—that tested whether or not a police lineup that included an indicted defendant should be admissible if the defendant's lawyer was not present. The Court ruled it should not be, judging that such a lineup was another "critical stage" where a person's right to counsel was essential. However, a 1968 law passed by Congress made a lineup identification made without the defendant's lawyer being present admissible in federal court. The Court itself, in the 1972 case *Kirby v. Illinois*, ruled that lineups that included a person who had been accused of a crime but not yet indicted were admissible.

The Right to Effective Aid

The right to counsel is meaningless if the attorney appointed to a defendant does not aid in the defendant's defense. Just having a lawyer sitting next to the accused person in court is not enough to satisfy the Sixth Amendment's protections. This was one of the reasons the Court overturned the convictions of the black men in the Scottsboro case—although a lawyer was with them during the trial, he had not prepared for the case and could do little to help them.

However, proving that a person's lawyer is incompetent—not skilled enough to provide a good legal defense—has proved very hard to do. Early tests of the concept of effective counsel focused on the problem of having one lawyer represent two defendants in the same case. The Supreme Court ruled in both 1942 and 1978 that this makes effective representation impossible, as one lawyer cannot defend the rights of more than one defendant in the same case. In normal situations, though, even after the *Gideon* decision, the Court has ruled that every person who is tried for a crime runs some risk of his or her lawyer making a mistake. For this reason, getting a conviction overturned based on mistakes made by a court-appointed lawyer is very difficult. However, the normal process of appealing a decision because of legal mistakes committed during the trial still applied.

In 1984, the Court made clear that in order to decide a person had been deprived of effective counsel, the errors made by his or her lawyer had to be severe. That year, the Court reversed an appeals court decision in *United States v. Cronic* that overturned a conviction because the defendant's lawyer did not have any criminal law experience (he was a real estate lawyer) and had only a short time to prepare his case.

10 Cruel and Unusual Punishment

In the previous chapters, we have discussed the rights an accused person has primarily during a trial, although several of those rights—the protection from self-incrimination and the right to counsel, for example—have been expanded to include the time before the person has been brought to trial. In this chapter, we will examine the Eighth Amendment's protection from cruel and unusual punishment—a protection that comes into play only after an accused person's trial, and then only if he or she is found guilty.

The Eighth Amendment to the Constitution declares that cruel and unusual punishment cannot be inflicted. This idea goes back to the English Bill of Rights of 1689, and its principle has long been observed in the civilized world. But deciding whether or not a punishment is "cruel and unusual" led the Court into one of the most controversial areas of American justice to an issue that continues to divide people to this day—the death penalty.

While the Eighth Amendment can be assumed to protect people against some of the more horrible punishments of the past—branding, drawing and quartering, burning alive at the stake—the Supreme Court has had to carefully create a standard to decide if lesser punishments violate the amendment's protection. One of the most important tests the Court has used is the idea that a punishment must be in line with the offense that it punishes. In other words, minor offenses cannot be punished with the penalties of harsher crimes. This principle was first decided in the 1910 case *Weems v. United States,* when the Court overturned a Philippine law (at the time, the Philippines were a U.S. territory) that punished lying on a public document with heavy fines and fifteen years of hard labor. The Court found that this penalty was not in line with the penalties for similar minor offenses or the penalties for more serious crimes, which could actually be less severe. This idea remains in practice today.

As with all the protections of the Bill of Rights, it took many years for the Eighth Amendment to be applied to the states. In a highly unusual case from 1947, the Court for the first time considered whether or not the Eighth Amendment could be used against a state. The case, *Louisiana ex rel. Francis v. Resweber* involved a prisoner, Willie Francis, who had been sentenced to death in the electric chair. When he was put in the chair and the switch that would send the current through his body, killing him, was thrown, an equipment failure occurred and his life was spared. He was then sent back to prison and made to wait for another execution. The Court rejected Francis's appeal that making him undergo a second execution was

Some opponents of capital punishment believe that the death penalty constitutes cruel and unusual punishment and is unconstitutional under the Eighth Amendment.

cruel, finding that there was no intent to cause him excess pain, but that a simple accident had prevented the machine from working the first time.

It was not until 1962 that the Eighth Amendment was finally extended to include the states. In the case of *Robinson v. California,* the Court struck down a California law that made being a drug addict a crime punishable by ninety days in jail. The Court found that, unlike other drug laws, the California law did not punish any act, but simply the condition of being addicted. Justice Potter Stewart dryly noted that punishment of even one day would be cruel and unusual for the "crime" of having a cold.

However, the Court refused the appeal of a man who argued that his conviction for public drunkenness was cruel and unusual because he was an alcoholic. In this case, the Court ruled that he was being punished only for being drunk in public—not for being an alcoholic.

The Court and Capital Punishment

As the curious *ex rel. Francis* case showed, the issues of capital punishment and cruel and unusual punishment have often been linked. Many death penalty opponents tried throughout the twentieth century to bring a case to the Supreme Court that would result in the Court declaring the death penalty to be unconstitutional under the Eighth Amendment. For many years, the Court dodged this issue by refusing to hear appeals based on this logic; its only statements on the death penalty were limited to questions about the juries in capital cases. However, in 1972 the Court heard the case of *Furman v. Georgia*. The decision was a legal bombshell: The death penalty was unconstitutional.

The Court was sharply divided over the issue, and the vote was only 5-4. An indication of how difficult it was to come to this decision was that each of the five justices who voted against the death penalty wrote his own opinion, rather than having one justice write a single opinion for them. Their opinions based their decisions on various factors, from Justice Thurgood Marshall's moral opposition to the death penalty to Justice Douglas's feeling that the death penalty law of Georgia was applied totally by whim and lacked guidelines that would make it fair. This line of reasoning was important because the death penalty was finally judged by the Court to be unconstitutional only in the manner it was then applied.

After the *Furman* decision, several states passed new death penalty laws that tried to correct the faults the Court had found with the Georgia law. They did this by one of two ways: either making the death penalty the only possible punishment for some crimes, or by allowing juries, in a special procedure called the penalty phase, to decide whether or not to give a person they had convicted the death penalty or instead give him or her another punishment—usually life in prison. These laws got around Justice Douglas's objections that there were no guidelines as to how and when the death penalty should be imposed.

In 1976, the Court reviewed these two kinds of laws. The most famous case it decided was *Gregg v. Georgia*. Georgia, following the *Furman* decision, had adopted a new series of laws that used the jury-decision method to impose the death penalty. In another 5-4 vote, the Court upheld this law, freeing the states to once again use the death penalty. That same day, however, in *Woodson v. North Carolina,* they struck down laws that made the death penalty the only punishment for certain kinds of crimes.

Over the next few years, the Court continued to clarify when the death penalty was not cruel or unusual punishment. In *Thompson v. Oklahoma* (1988), the court ruled that it was cruel to execute a person who had been only fifteen years old at the time of the crime. Later decisions established that sixteen was the minimum age that a person could be put to death.

Other decisions have found that it is not unconstitutional to execute a retarded person who was competent to be tried in the first place. However, the Court ruled that a state could not put to death a person who, although sane at the time of his or her trial, had since developed mental illness. The decision did mean that if he or she recovered from the illness and once again became competent, he or she could still be executed.

The Court has also held that it is constitutional for a person who is only an accomplice to a crime that carries the death penalty to be executed. However, in order for an accomplice to be executed, he or she must have played a major role in the crime and shown indifference to human life.

In the 1987 case of *McCleskey v. Kemp,* another attempt was made to make the death penalty unconstitutional because of the way it was applied. In another 5-4 decision, the Court once again upheld Georgia's death penalty laws, even though black people who had killed white people were four times as likely to be executed in the state as white people who had killed other white people. The Court decided that the disparity between black and white defendants did not necessarily prove that the law was being unfairly applied.

Even before the *Furman* decision, the Court had ruled on the question of whether a person who was opposed to the death penalty could be excluded from serving on a jury in a case that could result in it being applied. In *Witherspoon v. Illinois* (1968), the Court ruled that it was unconstitutional to exclude such a large group from jury selection. This had the effect of making it more difficult to convict a person of a death penalty offense.

This ruling began to be restricted starting in 1985 with the Court's ruling in *Wainwright v. Witt*. This allowed the exclusion of potential jurors who said that their opposition to the death penalty would cause a severe strain on their ability to act as jurors. However, more recent rulings have found that improper exclusion of a juror because of his or her beliefs about the death penalty justified a new trial for the defendant, and that it was constitutional for the defense to ask potential jurors if they would automatically apply the death penalty and exclude those people who said they would.

Other Aspects of the Protection from Cruel and Unusual Punishments

In recent years, there has been a movement in many states (and the federal government) to make long sentences mandatory, or the only possible punishment, for defendants who had been convicted of crimes they had been convicted of several times before. These repeat offender laws were eventually challenged as cruel and in violation of the Eighth Amendment.

The first test of this theory, *Rummel v. Estelle* (1980), found that it was not unconstitutional to give a person a mandatory life sentence if he or she had been convicted for three petty, nonviolent crimes. In 1983, however, this decision was reversed by *Solem v. Helm,* which found it was unconstitutional for a mandatory life sentence to be given to a person who had committed six previous non-violent offenses.

In 1977, the Court found that the Eighth Amendment did not protect children from corporal punishment—physical punishment, such as spanking—while in school, even though in the case the Court was reviewing, the child had been hit twenty times with a paddle and missed several days of school afterward. The Court's reasoning was that the open nature of the school system would prevent major abuses of corporal punishment.

11 Conclusion

The Constitution and the Bill of Rights have been great guardians of the liberty of Americans. United States citizens are guaranteed more freedom than almost any other people in the world. The clear, easy to understand language of both documents gives every citizen capable of reading the chance to understand his or her rights. Few societies in human history have been bold enough to create a document that says more about what the government cannot do than what it can; few others have also made a statement about the basic rights of their citizens and charged the government with protecting these rights and even enlarging them over time.

At the same time, while the Bill of Rights held out the promise of freedom for all Americans, for a long time many Americans were denied its basic protections. For the first seventy-eight years of its existence, the Constitution did not protect most African Americans because they were held in slavery. Even after slavery was outlawed, it took even longer for the promise of the Fourteenth Amendment—that the federal government would protect the rights of all citizens, even when the states they lived in tried to take them away—to be granted.

Throughout all of this time, the Supreme Court has continued to exercise its great power to judge the laws of the United States. The Supreme Court cannot make laws; it can only strike them down. But its ability to create clear guidelines as to what laws can be deemed constitutional has allowed it to have enormous influence on the ways laws are written and applied in the United States.

For most of the nineteenth and twentieth centuries, the Court exercised this ability very carefully, to the point of restricting the obvious meaning of the Fourteenth Amendment. However, as minorities in this country began to become more politically active and demand their rights, the Court emerged as a major force in combating historic injustices.

By denying accused people their rights, a government commits its greatest injustice. Cases such as the two Scottsboro ones and the *Miranda* case show how the power of the government can be abused. For this reason, the founders made the rights of the accused the subject of four of the ten amendments in the Bill of Rights.

Because of this, many of the most important cases decided by the Supreme Court have involved these rights. These decisions have often been controversial; many times, they have forever altered the way that the police and government must act in order to legally convict a person of a crime.

But the guiding principle has always remained the same: to prevent injustice and make the system as fair as possible. This has often resulted in making some groups unhappy.

The liberal Courts of the 1960s angered many who felt that their decisions were too easy on criminals and made it too difficult for the police and government to catch and punish lawbreakers. Likewise, some people today are worried that the more conservative Courts of the 1980s and early 1990s have gone too far in the other direction and have made the system less just and more likely to convict an innocent person.

Criminal justice is always a difficult subject. It is the ultimate test of a government that promises liberty to the people it governs. In a criminal trial, an individual is put into conflict with the government at the most basic level, for his or her liberty is put in danger by the very government that is charged to defend it. At the same time, a government needs to operate for the greatest benefit of all its citizens, and therefore must punish an individual who hurts, kills, or robs another person.

Especially in a democratic society, a trial not only tests the person who is accused of a crime but the government itself. For the government must obey its own rules, even if it means letting a guilty person go free, so that it may ensure that the innocent need not fear being punished for crimes they did not commit.

No system is perfect, and our system is no exception. People who are innocent are sometimes convicted. People who are guilty do sometimes get away with it. Yet few plans have worked better than the United States Constitution to protect both the liberty of ordinary people and the rights of those accused of a crime. It and the Bill of Rights remain to this day beacons of hope, promises that liberty and freedom are available to all who

Some of the most important and controversial cases decided by the Supreme Court have involved the rights of the accused.

enjoy the benefit of government "of the people, by the people, for the people."

The Constitution and the Bill of Rights are living documents. They do not stay the same, but grow and change over time. They are a part of our heritage, a hope for our future, a vital part of our everyday life.

Preamble to the Constitution

We the People of the United States, in order to form a more perfect Union, establish Justice, insure domestic Tranquility, provide for the common defence, promote the general Welfare, and secure the Blessings of Liberty to ourselves and our Posterity, do ordain and establish this Constitution for the United States of America.

On September 25, 1789, Congress transmitted to the state legislatures twelve proposed amendments, two of which, having to do with congressional representation and congressional pay, were not adopted. The remaining ten amendments became the Bill of Rights.

The Bill of Rights

Amendment I

Congress shall make no law respecting an establishment of religion, or prohibiting the free exercise thereof; or abridging the freedom of speech, or of the press; or the right of the people peaceably to assemble, and to petition the Government for a redress of grievances.

Amendment II

A well regulated Militia, being necessary to the security of a free State, the right of the people to keep and bear Arms, shall not be infringed.

Amendment III

No Soldier shall, in time of peace be quartered in any house, without the consent of the Owner, nor in time of war, but in a manner to be prescribed by law.

Amendment IV

The right of the people to be secure in their persons, houses, papers, and effects, against unreasonable searches and seizures, shall not be violated, and no Warrants shall issue, but upon probable cause, supported by Oath or affirmation, and particularly describing the place to be searched, and the persons or things to be seized.

Amendment V

No person shall be held to answer for a capital, or otherwise infamous crime, unless on a presentment or indictment of a Grand Jury, except in cases arising in the land or naval forces, or in the Militia, when in actual service in time of War or public danger; nor shall any person be subject for the same offence to be twice put in jeopardy of life or limb; nor shall be compelled in any criminal case to be a witness against himself, nor be deprived of life, liberty, or property, without due process of law; nor shall private property be taken for public use, without just compensation.

Amendment VI

In all criminal prosecutions, the accused shall enjoy the right to a speedy and public trial, by an impartial jury of the State and district wherein the crime shall have been committed, which district shall have been previously ascertained by law, and to be informed of the nature and cause of the accusation; to be confronted with the witnesses against him; to have compulsory process for obtaining witnesses in his favor, and to have the Assistance of Counsel for his defence.

Amendment VII

In Suits at common law, where the value in controversy shall exceed twenty dollars, the right of trial by jury shall be preserved, and no fact tried by a jury, shall be otherwise re-examined in any Court of the United States, than according to the rules of the common law.

Amendment VIII

Excessive bail shall not be required, nor excessive fines imposed, nor cruel and unusual punishments inflicted.

Amendment IX

The enumeration in the Constitution, of certain rights, shall not be construed to deny or disparage others retained by the people.

Amendment X

The powers not delegated to the United States by the Constitution, nor prohibited by it to the States, are reserved to the States respectively, or to the people.

Glossary

acquittal   The decision, either by a jury or a judge, that a person is not guilty of a crime for which he or she has been accused.

appeal   Asking a higher court to review the decision in a case and change it.

arraignment   The process of formally accusing a person of a crime before a judge and making him or her plead either guilty or not guilty to the charge.

capital case   A case involving a crime that carries the death penalty.

certiorari, writ of   Special order issued by the Supreme Court granting an appeal to it.

checks and balances   Fundamental principle behind the construction of the U.S. government. Each branch of government has specific powers granted to it. However, each other branch has the power to prevent that branch from abusing its power.

confession   Admission by a person that he or she is guilty of a crime.

conviction   Decision by a jury or a judge that a person is guilty of the crime he or she has been charged with.

counsel   A lawyer who assists a person in his or her defense.

defendant   In criminal cases, the person who has been indicted for a crime.

double jeopardy   Trying a person for a crime he or she has already been tried for.

due process   A promise that the government will create fair procedures for conducting trials and follow those procedures, even when it damages a case.

evidence   Any information that relates to whether or not a person has committed a crime. Evidence may be physical, such as blood samples, or consist of the testimony of witnesses or the opinion of experts about other evidence in the trial.

ex post facto   Latin for "after the fact"; in constitutional studies, writing a law that punishes a person for an action that was not a crime when it was made. Forbidden by the Constitution.

grand jury   From twelve to twenty-three citizens who determine if there is probable cause that a person has committed a crime. If they find probable cause, they can then issue an indictment. Required for all major federal offenses under the Fifth Amendment; states are not required to use them, and many do not.

immunity   A guarantee that a person will not be prosecuted. Often granted in exchange for testimony.

incorporation   In constitutional studies, the expansion of the rights guaranteed by the Bill of Rights to apply to actions taken by the states, not just the federal government. When this occurs, the right is said to have been "incorporated against the states." Incorporation of much of the Bill of Rights was the result of several highly controversial Supreme Court decisions in the 1960s.

indictment   A formal statement accusing a person of a crime, issued by the government, and necessary in most cases before a criminal trial can begin.

jurisdiction   The power of a court to hear a specific case. Courts are limited to the kinds of cases they can hear by the laws of the government.

legislature   A body of the government that has the ability to make laws.

overturn   To change the decision of a lower court or a precedent.

petit jury/trial jury   The jury that decides during a trial whether or not the charges brought against someone are true.

probable cause   Reasonable belief, based on the evidence presented, that a person has committed a crime. Necessary in order to obtain an indictment.

reverse   To change the ruling of a lower court or a precedent to its opposite decision.

suspect   A person believed to have committed a crime, but who has not yet been indicted.

testimony   The statements of a witness during a trial.

waive   To give up a right or privilege.

For More Information

http://www.law.cornell.edu
Cornell Law School's Web site provides all Supreme
Court decisions since 1990 and more than fifty cases
of historic interest.

http://oyez.at.nwu.edu/oyez.html
Northwestern University provides this service, which
has RealAudio recordings of oral arguments before the
Supreme Court.

http://www.supremecourtus.gov
Official Web site of the U.S. Supreme Court.

http://www.law.emory.edu
Emory University School of Law's Web site allows
searches of the U.S. Constitution and has links to
other law sites and the various branches of the
U.S. government.

http://www.yale.edu/lawweb/avalon/avalon.htm
The Avalon Project at the Yale Law School Web site
contains important documents from U.S. history,
including the Constitution, the Articles of
Confederation and treaties and letters.

http://www.nara.gov
The National Archives site is home to not only the
Constitution but also to searchable databases of
presidential papers and many other features.

For Further Reading

Abernathy, M. Glenn. *Civil Liberties Under the Constitution*. Columbia, SC: University of South Carolina Press, 1989.

Alderman, Ellen, and Caroline Kennedy. *In Our Defense: The Bill of Rights in Action*. New York: Morrow, 1991.

Amar, Akhil R. *The Bill of Rights: Creation and Reconstruction*. New Haven, CT: Yale University Press, 1998.

Biskupic, Joan, and Elder Witt. *The Supreme Court and Individual Rights*. 3rd ed. Washington, DC: Congressional Quarterly, Inc., 1997.

Bodenhamer, David J. *Fair Trial: Rights of the Accused in American History*. New York: Oxford University Press, 1992.

Hickok, Eugene W., Jr., ed. *The Bill of Rights: Original Meaning and Current Understanding*. Charlottesville, VA: University Press of Virginia, 1991.

Kukla, Jon, ed. *The Bill of Rights: A Lively Heritage.* Richmond, VA: Virginia State Library and Archives, 1987.

Levy, Leonard W. *Original Intent and the Framer's Constitution.* Chicago: Ivan R. Dee, 2000.

Lieberman, Jethro K. *A Practical Companion to the Constitution: How the Supreme Court Has Ruled on Issues from Abortion to Zoning.* Berkley, CA: University of California Press, 1999.

Nagel, Stuart S., ed. *The Rights of the Accused in Law and Action.* Beverly Hills: Sage Publications, 1972.

Riley, Gail Blasser. *Miranda v. Arizona: Rights of the Accused.* Hillside, NJ: Enslow Publishers, 1994.

Index

Photo Credits

Cover: The Constitution of the United States of America; pp. 8, 12, 15, 35, 38, 41, 51, 55, 59, 61, 75, 80, 94, 104 © Corbis; p. 17 © Marc Muench/Corbis; pp. 20, 29 © Archive Photo; p. 23 © Michael J. Pettypool/Pictor; pp. 31, 70, 85 © AP/Wide World Photos; pp. 43, 113 © Pictor; p. 62 © Wally McNamee/Corbis; p. 99 © The Everett Collection.

Series Design
Danielle Goldblatt

Layout
Les Kanturek